MOMENTS WITH MANCLARK

Poetry written by
Dave Manclark
97 Glenvarloch Crescent
Edinburgh EH16 6BB

Illustrated by George Leslie

First published 1988
by
The Amaising Publishing House Ltd
(Scotprint Ltd)
P.O. Box
Musselburgh
EH21 7UJ
Scotland
031-665 6767

ISBN 1 871512 00 X

MOMENTS WITH MANCLARK

The Amaising Publishing House Ltd
Musselburgh

This Book is dedicated to my two Grandchildren
Kirsty and Lawrie

FOREWORD

In response to many requests from friends and the public alike, and after many unsuccessful attempts to find a publisher, finally, through the kind auspices of a friend, Charlie Watt of Scotprint Ltd in Musselburgh, this bagatelle of poems 'Moments with Manclark,' have been rescued from the dusty shelves of infinite obscurity.

Old favourites have been included by request, as previous editions have either been lent or lost, so may I kindly advise the reader, 'Neither a borrower nor a lender be,' in so far as this edition is concerned.

I can only hope that the reader will get as much enjoyment out of these poems, as I have had when writing or reciting them. May I also take this opportunity to thank everyone for their help and advice, and also in their continuing interest in poetry.

David F. Manclark

CONTENTS

Poem—Continued | *Page*

AULD LEITH IS NO' THE SAME MAN

Aye, Auld Leith will never be the same again, the Edinburgh Council and the City Planners, have torn the heart out of this once bustling Community. They did more damage than the German Bombers during World War II, and only now have realised their mistake. Like all 'Leithers' I remember the times I spent as a laddie in Leith.

I was born an' bred in Sunny Leith
A fact of which I'm proud man
On pure whalebone I cut my teeth
And bawled my lungs full well man

Raised on tripe and potted heid
On stovies, haugh, and ribs man
At school I learnt tae write an' read
Wi' wooden pens, Wi' nibs man

My Faither was a Merchant Man
An' sailed the World wide man
Fae Port o' Leith tae far Japan
And never missed a tide man

Our hoose was jist a 'but an' ben'
The fender made o' brass man
The grate was zebo-ed once a week
An' the hoose was lit by gas man

Wi' stippled walls and ceilings high
The colours a' would blend man
Tho' money was in short supply
Your neighbour was your friend man

I've bawled up for a piece-an-jam
And caught it in full flight man
I've built a 'Guider' oot a pram
Doon the Links I've flown a kite man

While lassies played at 'Peevry-Beds'
Or sang the Skippin' Rhymes man
The laddies played at 'Pitchin' Toss'
Or 'Keepy-up' in lines man

I've caw'd a 'Gird' at quite a speed
And whipped a 'Peery' well man
I've heard advice an' ta'en nae heed
And payed the price full well man

I've sat in 'The Gods' in the 'Alabam'
Slid doon the 'Giant's Brae' man
I've been tae 'Porty' on a tram
Mair times than I can tell man

These days are gone, and so's our hoose
On which we staked our claim man
Wi' planners playin' fast and loose
Auld Leith is no' the same man

THE LOST RACE

A lawyer in an English Court, stated that a Scotsman could not claim discrimination as there was no Nation called Scotland.

This Land is ours, by Charter set
And Heroes aye respected
Alas today, we now forget
And our History lies neglected

Once a proud and worthy Race
That bore their Name with pride
Who met the 'Devil' face to face
And took him in their stride

Bewitched, betrayed, by so called Peers
And sold for personal gain
Brainwashed for so many years
Now treated with disdain

What once has been, can happen twice
Be proud to take your part
Avoid the silver tongued advice
The gold is in the heart

Be aware o' what's around you
Take a pride in what you see
Your History stands behind you
Control your destiny
We're used, abused, sometimes confused
Yet never put to shame
Aye Scotland is a Nation
And that Nation is our hame

THE STIPPLED WA'

The walls in nearly every house in Leith, when I was a laddie, were stippled with distemper. The method was, to use a sponge or cloth, and two or more different colours. To me it was a form of art, to my parents, it was the cheapest form of wall decoration.

As a boy, I'd lie in bed
And gaze at the stippled wa'
Shapes and forms, would come alive
From the sponge marks big and sma'

Horses pranced, and devils danced
In the flickering mantle light
A hand, a claw, a furry paw
An eagle in full flight

I'd shift my eyes still further on
Select another space
And there below the ceiling
A bearded unknown face

And there, a figure, spear in hand
Poised, tae make a lunge
And all these figures given life
By my faither's magic sponge

Aye Rembrandt and Picasso
Painted pictures that were braw
But nothing like that bed-recess
And my faither's stippled wa'

CHILDHOOD GAMES

Gone are the days when a' the weans
Played the game o' 'Chuckie Stanes'
Or strung 'Diablo's' tae the sky
An' caught them on their sticks raised high

Or chalkin' 'Beds' on pavin' slate
An' skiffing 'Peever Tins' sae straight
Or whippin' 'PEERIES' like the Deil
Or runnin' wi' their 'Girds' o' steel

Or singin' 'Skippin' Rhymes' sae braw
Each takin' turns tae skip or caw
Gone, like the water doon the burn
And lost in the sea of no return

THE BELLES O' AULD NEWHAVEN

Dedicated to the Womens Senior Citizen's Club which meet in the Madras Hall, in Craighall Road, Newhaven.

When cauld winds blaw across the Forth
And sanctuary you're cravin'
Then chap the door o' Madras Hall
In the Kirkyard o' Newhaven

For there within a welcome lies
And what they have they're sharin'
You'll maybe even win a prize
Fae the Belles o' Auld Newhaven

A' senior lassies in their prime
Wi' hearts brimfu' o' carin'
They'd charm the birds of a' the trees
The Belles o' Auld Newhaven

They'll sing o' 'Buckie Wives' wi' creels
And shoals o' 'Caller Herrin'
The sangs o' Guid Auld Scotia's past
The Belles o' Auld Newhaven

If e'er weighed doon wi' wordly care
And harmony yer cravin'
Jist daunder doon tae Craighall Kirk
And meet the Belles o' Auld Newhaven

ON LEAVING SCHOOL

This is a satirical look at the situation that the average school leavers find themselves in today. They leave school with high hopes seeking employment, then realise that it can be months, sometimes even years before they are usefully employed. This is frustrating and also a deplorable situation.

You've reached sixteen now laddie
It's time tae put aside your toys
And step intae the outside world
Tae join the 'Dole Queue Boys'

It's a growing organisation
Separate from your Dad's
I'm sure you'll grow tae like it
Just like all the lads

Don't worry about working
Our system works a treat
Think of all the leisure time
You'll have tae roam the street

You neednae rise each morning
Tae face a tiring day
Only fools work tae the rules
Apathy rules. . . . O.K.

We'll send your money to you
Once you've joined our 'Cleek'
If you'll just sign, the dotted line
Once in every week

Aye sign up wi' our legions lad
Don't pause tae even think
For the working man, like the Dodo clan
Will soon become extinct

So drop in soon and see us laddie
We'll all be overjoyed
And by signing on the dotted line
You'll keep 'US' all employed

ABERDOUR

I've spent many a pleasing summer hour
On the 'Silver Sands' o' Aberdour
Watching the bairns enjoy their play
In that warm and sunny horseshoe bay

THE CHALLENGE

It is in the nature of man, no matter what his circumstances in life are, he'll always meet a challenge, below, is one such challenge.

Auld Harry was a docker
Whae worked the Port o' Leith
A cheery minded joker,
But a cheeky minded thief

Now on The Gate, was Brocky
A man whae loved his work
So arrogant and cocky
And tighter than a cork
He'd stand there proudly at his post
His glinting eyes would flash
An' Brocky always made the boast
That nae contraband would pass

One day he saw Auld Harry
Stroll up to his gate
Pushing an empty 'barry'
Prepared tae meet his fate

His piercing eyes searched Harry's face
For a trace o' guilt or fear
But Harry stood there, full o' grace
Ignoring Brocky's leer

The Eyes then searched the 'barry'
But couldnae find a bean
So he grunted tae Auld Harry
'O.K. this time your clean'

Brocky let Auld Harry through
Still giving his piercing stare
Like the cat at the chip shop windae, thought
There's something fishy there

Now many times throughout the years
They acted out this scene
But the 'barry' was always empty
And Auld Harry was always clean

Auld Harry is retired now
And sits as happy as a cub
In that plushy pillared paradise
They call The Dockers Club

One day in walked Brocky
And sat down near in tears
'I've got tae ask ye Harry
For it's been botherin' me for years
What exactly were ye stealing?
Don't lie now, tell me true'
'It was the 'Barries', Brocky, 'Barries'
And ye always let me through'

Some men cross the Continents
With a Bible and a Prayer
Some climb the highest mountains
Just because they're there
They'll always meet the 'Challenge'
And try and 'beat the clock'
That's why there's nae contentment, Brocky
And nae Barries, in the Dock.

NIGHT AND DAY

When night's ghostly armies
Creep with noiseless tread
Advancing, on the rearguards of light
That, is night

When the crusading streaks of sunlight
Pierce the ranks of darkness
And the grey shadows, retreat and melt away
That, is day.

THE PRESTONPANS PLATE-FY

I was invited to the annual 'Burns Supper' at Prestonpans, and thoroughly enjoyed myself, (as I do at all Burns Nights) but what left a lasting impression on me, was the meal. It had me spread-eagled on my chair, 'Blawin' for the Tugs'. The Speakers and the Artists were excellent, and the hospitality was tremendous, in all, what you might term a 'Rare Nicht'.

I was asked tae the 'Mystic Burns Supper'
Held at the Thorntree Hall
A night I'll always remember
And one I'll always recall

I've supped at many a table
Wi' a' the 'Cleeks an' the Clans'
But they a' take the second o' prizes
Tae that 'Plate-fy' at Auld Prestonpans

Steak Pie, Tatties, and Tumshie
The Haggis, it lay there in state
A crusty brown pastry, and gravy
Smothered the Prestonpans Plate

Muckin' in tae that braw Scottish Dinner
Not a trace did I leave there in sight
Then the buttons popped off o' my braces
As up swoll my overfilled kyte

Let them talk o' their goulash an' chinky
Zipped in their dry tasteless flans
But gie me that man-sized heap plate-fy
That they serve doon in Auld Prestonpans

Tae a' you Burns lovers at Thorntree
I'll aye stand clappin' my hands
For a night I'll always remember
The 'Burns Night' at Auld Prestonpans

A WEE LADDIE'S GRACE

I was a wee laddie once, and this is how I felt sometimes, and I think all wee laddies do.

When we sit down at mealtimes Lord
I always get the smallest bit
So bless this hungry laddie Lord
And see if You can double it.

THE GOLD RUSH (1980)

January, 1980, saw the price of gold zoom upwards to an all time record, many people were either selling it, or buying it in the hope that it would go even higher. It seems like the very mention of the word gold, can still drive people a little crazy, I wonder what would happen if the price plummeted to an all time low.

Not since the days o' the 'Gold Rush'
When Chaplin ate his auld boot
And a' the roads led tae the 'Klondyke'
Where they dug for that soft yellow root

In every wee hoose in the Country
They're rakin' oot cupboards and drawers
Or rummagin' through a' their attics
An' doon under beds on all fours

The housewife tae has went crazy
When prices are taken tae task
'Tae hell wi' the price o' the butter
How much is a Sovereign', they'll ask

One woman ran hame tae her guid man
An' clattered him one on the jaw
'That ring ye gave me's gold plated
An' no' eighteen carats at a''

Another wife louped at her husband
Her legs caught his neck in a hold
She pulled his jaws near asunder
Just tae see if his fillings were gold

They're queueing outside a' the pawnshops
Redeeming their silver and gold
Then hurrying hame tae their cache
It's a humourous sight tae behold

Aye gold is the language they're speaking
As they count every carat and grain
Tho' you don't need a pick and a shovel
The 'Gold Rush' is on once again.

DONER
KEBABS
CURRIES
ZZIAS

THE NEW REEK

Auld Reekie, as Edinburgh is sometimes called, was like most major cities, full of tenements and heavy industry, and the main fuel was coal. Before the Pollution Laws came into force a blanket of smoke or smog used to hang over the city, hence the name 'Auld Reekie'. In the last ten years or so, the amount of Chinese and Indian restaurants has grown immensely, giving Edinburgh a new reek.

Sniff the wind guid neighbour
Nae mair will ye cough and choke
Wi' pollution laws and smokeless fuel
Auld Reekie's lost her smoke

Look at the sky guid neighbour
Any hour of the day or week
Nae mair will the Fifers tell the time
By our chimneys spirlin' reek

But haud yer breath guid neighbour
There's a new reek waftin' bye
O' hungry folks wi' curry pokes
And smells o' Auld Shanghai

Auld Reekie's turned gey Chinky
And followed the Hong Kong craze
Wi' curried roots and bamboo shoots
And Chinese take-aways

There's other scents that pinch yer nose
On the City's wind o' change
The reek o' Indian spices
Fae the Eastern cookin' range

Nae mair the clouds o' reekin' soot
That hung like a widow's veil
Covering everything in sight
Wi' it's black and grimy scale

Aye there's a new reek now guid neighbour
That hangs around our streets
O' strange exotic dishes
And oriental treats

So fill yer lungs guid neighbour
And savour the treats galore
It's full o' Eastern Promise
Auld Reekie reeks once more

PETER THE METER

This is a story which takes place in the Royal Mile in Edinburgh. This famous street runs from Edinburgh Castle down to Holyrood Palace, and is steeped in Scottish History and many books have been written on it's history and characters. I found myself walking this street late one night, and my imagination began to run riot. The reference to 'Proddy John' (John Knox) taking his nightly walk, is pure fiction, as is Burke and Hare the murderers, or is it? The Morrocan Prince, is a character in the history of the Canongate, the Yellow Peril are the Traffic Wardens.

Some stories now, you may have read
While lying safely in yer bed
Or snugged cosy, in yer chair
Stories, that wid curl yer hair
Or make yer heart go tic-a-tac
Or the hackles rise oot on yer back

The story I'm about tae tell
Lately, on a night befell
I must admit I'd had a few
O' my favourite, tattie-peelin' brew
The moon wis oot, and the hour wis late
When I came roon, by the Canongate
Oot o' breath, I paused awhile
And gazed up that ghostly Royal Mile

A Street, where Kings an' Queens parade
Fae the Palace, tae The Esplanade
Where old and new stand side by side
A Street that fills us a' wi' pride
By day, sae bustly and sae cheery
At night, sae ghostly and sae eerie

Well up this street, I took tae wind
Three steps foritt, an' two behind
An' halfway up, I took a teeter
And grabbed a haud o' a parking meter
'Steady up', I heard someone say
I looked aroun' in great dismay
Not a soul in sight, the place wis deid
An' my brain went birlin' in my heid

A ghost I thought, aye it's Proddy John
Oot for a walk, before the dawn
Or the Morrocan Prince, clawn oot the soil
Come tae claim, Auld Scotland's Oil
Or the body-snatchin' Burke an' Hare
Trying tae catch me unaware
'Whae's there?' says I, trying tae smile
'Jist me, sit doon and rest awhile'
I staggered back, and stood there gawkin'
It wis the Parkin' Meter talking

I wiped the sweat fae off my broo
It wis like somethin' oot o' Doctor Who
'Do ye have a name, are ye friend or foe?'
'Aye, Peter the Meter, naw dinnae go
It's ages since I had a chatter
Come on, sit doon and gies yer patter
Have ye got 10p, I'd be awfy gled
It's hours since, I last wis fed'

I dropped the coin, in the slot provided
It 'burped' it's thanks, and then confided
'Ye Humans arnae a' that bad
Ye feed us a', and for that we're glad
But in a' the years, since I've been planted
Some o' ye take us a' for granted
Ye park yer cars, and pay yer fare
When time runs oot, ye curse and swear
It's no' us tae blame, it's the Yellow Peril
The 'Guid Book' said, they'd rule the world'

'Watch them dae their dance o' glee
When they catch a driver, parking free
Up in the air, their heels they clicket
Then slap yer windscreen wi' a ticket
And the yellow band, around their hat
That means ye cannae park on that'

I sat there listening, forgetting time
Until I heard the Third Hour chime
I said goodnight, then started walking
Leaving Peter there, still talking
An' thinking back, it's nae surprise
I hadnae got a word in, edgewise

But now I understand his plight
It must be lonely there at night
So when I park next tae a meter
I always think o' my chat wi' Peter
I feed the coin, and gie a smile
Remembering that night in the Royal Mile
So remember, meters arnae mugs
And by the way, THEY A' HATE DUGS.

DAVIE'S NAE MAIR

Auld Leith will never be the same
She's lost a Son o' High Acclaim
We'll never see his like again
On that I'll swear
She's sorrowed now in grief an' pain
Her Davie's nae mair

There's many a 'Hoose' his face has blessed
There's many 'Freend' he has impressed
Many's the time he's stood the test
Wi' burdens sair
Sadly now he takes his rest
Auld Davie's nae mair

God rest his soul, and the Heavens tent him
That's the wish o' a' that kent him
We bless the Shining Star that lent him
Wi' loving care
But now another road she's sent him
Our Davie's nae mair.

THE BACKGREEN SUNBATHER

Sandy McCann, was a down tae earth man
Whae worked hard a' the year round
When his holidays came, he aye stayed at hame
In the Backgreen he'd always be found

A table and chair, he needed nae mair
A bottle o' rum an' two cokes
He'd sit like a king, daen his ain thing
In his semmit, his bunnet, and flourescent socks

'Why should I fly tae Majorky' he'd cry
'Or drink vino an' bubbly champagne
I can sit here and rest, wi' a gless o' the best
And it's safer getting pissed here at hame'

But Bessie his wife, the love o' his life
Aye yearned for a holiday abroad
So she pestered her man, tae take her on wan
And Sandy was as good as his word

They flew off tae Spain, without too much pain
And landed in Lloret de Mar
They liked the hotel, the room tae was swell
And so was the fancy big bar

Sandy arranged, tae go up and get changed
While Bess took a jaunt round the shops
And when she came back, her pride took a whack
At the sight on the hotel's front slopes

For sitting in view, wi' table an' pew
Wi' a flagon o' rum an' two cokes
Was Sandy her dear, dressed up in his gear
O' Semmit, an' Bunnet, an' Flourescent Socks

A FISHY TALE

Man has now trained Dolphins to do many clever things, but an item in the local newspaper showed how far man would really go to further his own ends., A report from America claimed that they were now training Dolphins to kill frogmen, by strapping laser guns, and stun guns, to them in order to protect their underwater security. This inspired the following tale.

The strangest thing has happened man
In the world beneath the sea
Auld Neptune's lost his Kingdom
And fled tae the Zeider Zee

And in his place upon the throne
Complete with laser gun
There sits Dick the Dolphin
Public Enemy Number One

In an upturned wreck, on the ocean floor
This killer rules the waves
And Dick and all his henchmen
Treat the other fish like slaves

There's Piranah Pete, and Gummy Shark
And eel called Slippery Sam
There's Jack the Kipper, the Swordfish Ripper
And a whale called Tam the Ram

There's 'Wanted' posters round their Howff
For humans we all know
Men like Captain Birdseye
And the Frenchy Jac' Cousteau

What made this friendly Dolphin kill
And bear the mark o' Cain
The answer's very simple friend
Man interfered again

He taught the Dolphins many tricks
With hoops and water games
And the Dolphins all responded well
For Dolphins too have brains

Then the crazy side o' man took ower
Teaching a deadly skill
With laser guns and poisoned spears
He taught them how to kill

The Dolphins picked up other things
Like greed and the lust for power
And once they were back in the Murky Deep
The Dolphins then took ower

Then things began tae happen
Strange accidents at sea
Could it be the Dolphins
It's still a mystery

So if you go out fishing
And your waiting on a bite
Make sure the Killer Dolphins
Arnae prowling there that night

When Mother Nature, rights all wrongs
After Man has had his way
He'll maybe learn, to conserve all life
And not destroy it every day.

QUESTION AND ANSWER

What is worn beneath a kilt
They'll question one another
Wi' smirks and sneers
And cynical leers
Ye wonder why they bother

But truth tae tell
WE a' ken well
Fae Caithness tae the Border
There's nothing worn beneath a kilt
It's all in working order.

THE WALLACE

Regrettably, many Scots have never read the life story William Wallace, and more regrettably, his life and struggle, fighting for the Independence of Scotland, is hardly mentioned or taught in our schools today. He was a great Scottish hero and patriot, and was the first to rise against the English in the Wars of Independence. He dedicated his life solely to the fight for Freedom, he signed no truces, accepted no bribes, and it's ironic to think that it was the Nobility of Scotland who first of all deserted him, then betrayed him for a price. He was finally caught and butchered by Edward I, but he still remains to many people, including myself, as un-questionably the greatest Scottish hero in our history.

Auld Scotia's bred some heroes bold
And o' their deeds, tales have been told
O' Stewarts, Black Douglas, and The Bruce
(Who sometimes fought or signed a truce)
And then one day at Bannockburn
Bruce stood fast and took his turn
Wi' horses, troops, and swords a' ready
Fairly skeplit Young King Eddy
All heroes great, yet none could fill
The socks or boots, o' Guardian Wull

Twas in the year Twelve-Ninety-One
That Wullie's troubles first began
The Wallace family had tae run
Or bear the gree
'You'll sign The Roll' was Edward's cry
Wullie's faither wid rather die
And afore King Eddy reasoned why
They fled tae Dundee

Twas here Wull's name began tae grow
An' caused the English grief and woe
He'd strike them doon, twa at a blow
Then leave them fair dumfoonered
His faither bravely killed at Ayr
Made our Wullie's heart sae sair,
He swore he'd lay Auld Scotland bare
Than gie it tae King Eddy

When Edward crowned our 'Puppet John'
Nae respect tae him was shown
When hate and discontent had grown
The 'Butcher' marched on Berwick
The English horde, he turned it loose
And made the Toon a slaughter hoose
He never even raised his broos
As they murdered bairns and women

It was Good Friday, and mark that date
The day that BERWICK met her fate
The day that Scotsmen began their hate
But nane as deep as Wullie
The 'Hoodie' Eddy and his carrion
Laid the Country bare and barren
And a' the Scots Lords, Peers and Barons
Swore him allegiance
Then hame rode Ed in great procession
The 'Stone o' Scone' in his possession

But in Ettrick Forest oot o' sight
Wallace broo'd Auld Scotia's plight
He swore he'd still keep up the fight
For his Country's Independence
Fae farms, and crofts, and toons and ports
He gathered men o' a' the sorts
Trained them tae a fighting force
Then proudly led them

His deed o' bravery soon spread
And in his wake, the English dead
Fae the barns o' Ayr, tae Biggar Field
He made the English turn or yield
Wi' his Twa-hand Sword, and massive shield
He sent them running

Now Bruce an' a' his cronies
And that devil ca'd Red Comyn
A' jined up wi' oor Guid Wull
For Battles he was winning
They swore they'd fight
For Scotland's Right
And send the English running

Meanwhile Ted the Ned, lay on his bed
In London Town, a-dreamin'
When in there rushed a lackey man
A-shoutin' an a-screamin'
'They bloody Scots, hae pulled up their socks
And are swearing they'll hae vengeance
They'll keep going till they drop
Tae get their Independence'.

'Now keep the heid', King Eddy said
'I'll show thae Scots nae mercy'
He sent oot forty thousand men
Under Clifford and Lord Percy
The two armies met, no' far fae IRVINE
The Scots well placed, but the Nobles girnin'
And Percy sat there fair amused
Watchin' the Scots get a' confused

'Red Comyn he'll lead', 'Naw we want Bruce'
Others shouted, 'Sign a truce'
'Guid Wallace, he's got plenty sass'
'But he's not of the Noble Class'
Quo' Wull, 'I'll no' sign Eddy's Papers
Tae me ye're jist a bunch o' traitors'
Then watched them a' wi' heids a' bent
Sign King Eddy's Document

Wallace left, and headed North
Wi' gallant Andy Moray
And a' the Scots that jined them
Went lookin' for a foray
They chased the English oot Montrose
Oot Forfar, and oot Brechin
And had King Eddy on his Throne
A-squirmin' an' a-squeakin'

Guid Wallace, aboot tae take Dundee
His men in siege lay waitin'
When news came o' the enemy
That really was breathtakin'
An army under Surrey
Wi' banners a'a-birlin'
Had come up fae the South
Intent tae march on Stirling

Wallace didnae hang aboot
But marched for a' his worth
Tae catch the English army
Before they crossed the Forth
Arrivin' there, wi' time tae spare
He weighed the situation
And there and then, he telt his men
'There's nae Capitulation'

Lord Surrey sent two friars oot
Wi' a message tae oor Wull
'Surrender now, gie up your fight
And come doon fae the hill'
Wallaced laughed, an' answered back
So everybody heard
'Tell them tae come oot an' fight
We'll meet them beard tae beard'

The English, under Cressingham
King Edward's Loyal Treasure Man
Who'd taxed the Scots, for many years
A mean an' really violent man
Began their march across The Brig
A move that proved ill-fated
For high up on the Abbey Craig
Wallace watched and waited

He seemed tae count them as they crossed
On that September morn
And when he thought enough had passed
He up an' blew his horn

The Scots wi' hearts a' full o' hate
Swept doon like rivers in full spate
Nae quarter asked, nae quarter sought
Wi' wild ferocity they fought
Till Edward's Banners lay in the mud
Soakin' in the English blood
And Cressingham was left a-hint
Not only dead, but also skint
Lord Surrey, seeing his army beat
Fled back tae Berwick, in defeat

Wallace now, wi' a' his band
Drove the English fae the land
Wi' thousands fighting by his side
He gave Auld Scotland back her pride
Fae Carlisle, tae Newcastle Gate
The Scots let loose their pent up hate
Then Wallace led his army hame
Tho' poor in wealth, gey rich in fame

Once hame, he wisnae one tae idle
He soon took up Auld Scotia's bridle
As GUARDIAN, a' his plans were bold
He broke the Nobles powerful hold
Took Scotland fae their greedy lap
And put her name back on the map
Then sent the word across the sea
Scotland once again was free

King Edward wanted Guid Wull deid
And put a price upon his heid
Then led an army at full speed
The Deil himsel' was in the lead
And jist ootside o' Falkirk Toon
This massive army bedded doon

'Tis said that night, tho' it could be fibs
A horse kicked two o' Eddy's ribs
The poet's note, in nae offence
The cuddy showed some guid horse-sense

Meanwhile, Wallace turning round
Decided that he'd stand his ground
He formed the Scots in Schiltroms weel
Like hedgehogs wi' their quills o' steel
And tho' outnumbered three tae one
Wallace knew they'd never run
The Scots now standing firm and steady
Waited on the charge o' Eddy

And charge they did, without delay
Fae left and right, wi' cavalry
But Spearmen stood like rocks that day
Turning their charge like broken spray
In circles formed like human dykes
A double row o' twelve-foot spikes
And Wallace fighting at their side
Let loose a 'Battle-Cry' o' pride

But Guid Wull's pride, then turned tae woe
He saw the crafty Comyn go
And with him went his cavalry
Having never struck a blow that day
The Spearmen left without support
Still stood their ground like bristled forts

When Eddy saw the 'Horse' desert
It fairly gladdened up his heart
His long-bow shafts did loudly rattle
The first time used in any battle
Guid Wallace, sickened tae his soul
Watched the archers take their toll
'HOW' he cried, in great dismay
'Do you kill a man a hundred yards away'
And gathering as many as he could
Retreated back intae the wood

He grieved for a' the men that fell
Until the tears began tae swell
The Stewart men, Grahams, and Macduff
Who on the field, had proved their worth
And the Nameless Ones, who'd taen their parts
Defying Edward's feathered darts
And on their names, Wull took his pause
And vowed he'd fight on for their cause

His 'GUARDIANSHIP' he now withdrew
And gave it back tae the 'Noble Crew'
He watched them as they fought anew
On whae was going tae govern
At last they chose not one, but two
Bruce, and the fox Red Comyn

Guid Wallace said, 'Dae as ye must
But I fight wi' men, that I can trust
And on our swords, you'll find nae rust
Till Scotland's free
For a' the gold, on this earthly crust
Can't buy my liberty'

Wallace for the next six years an' mair
Ran the English army sair
Had Eddy pullin' at his hair
In sheer frustration
For Wull was the only one still free
From English domination

But a' great things come tae a close
And Wullie's fight, was one o' those
Twas John Menteith, that did disclose
Our hero's hideaway
That Judas Scot, (may his bones a' rot),
Turned him in that day

They dragged Guid Wull tae London Town
And chained him where he lay
Wallace calmly waited trial
In 'Minster Hall next day
The next day dawned, as a' days do
Wallace named it as his last
The 'Trial' he was taken to
Was nothing but a farce

'You claim you're King of Scotland
And in that land ye rule
Well we crown ye wi' these laurels
And for your throne, a stool
You're a traitor tae King Edward
And his subjects, you did kill
You're jist a common robber
And it's time tae foot the bill'

Wallace stood and answered
In a voice baith loud and clear
It was the Voice of Scotland
With never a trace of fear
'Tae Edward I'm nae traitor
It's ower England, he is King
I've never paid him homage
He knows I'd rather swing
As tae slaying a' his subjects
I admit tae quite a few
They were invaders o' my country
And got what they were due'

The 'judges' then passed sentence
Fair justice they did cheat
They chained Wallace tae a hurdie
And dragged him through the street
Huge crowds around him gathered
They came fae a' the sorts
And couldnae help admire
The Guardian o' the Scots
At last they reached the gallows
Built special for our man
They hung him by the neck, and then
Their butchery began

They cut him down, still living
Disembowelled him where he lay
And the life o' William Wallace
Began tae drain away
Burning a' his innards, Wallace now was deid
They sliced his body intae four
And severed off his heid

They spiked his heid, on London Brig
A heid once proud and fine
The arm that held the 'Mighty Sword'
Spiked on the brig at Tyne
The arm that held the 'Famous Shield'
Spiked at Stirling in the North
His left leg spiked at Berwick
And his right leg spiked at Forth

Thus died William Wallace
Cut down in his prime
The Greatest Scottish Hero
O' this, or any time.

AMIN YOUR OOT

The President of Uganda, Idi Amin, announced publicly that he would be prepared to come to Scotland, be crowned King of Scotland, then lead us in our fight for Independence. The answer is below.

Idi Amin's no content
With his role o' President
And his medals hung in rows, across his chest
He's wantin' one mair thing
And that's tae be a King
The King o' a' The Scots, an' nothing less

But Idi, Idi, Idi
Ye must be off yer heidy
If you think you'll ever be, The King o' Scotland
On yer heid ye maybe carry
The famous Diced Glengarry
But tae be our Lawful King, ye've not a hope man

Since Thirteen Twenty-Nine
The days o' Auld Lang Syne
When Scotsmen aye were proud, an' brave, an' gallus
We've been waiting on a King
That would make this Country sing
Someone in the mould o' Bruce or Wallace

Tho' I must admire your choice
We Scots nae longer hae a Voice
On whae will rule this famous Land of ours
But may I say, 'Big Daddy'
It would be a Scottish Laddie
For we've seen and heard enough, o' Foreign Powers

But if ye have tae dae your thing
In Uganda, be a King
And fly your Standard high, from every steeple
Let freedom, be your goal
Don't let greed take ower yer soul
And let your Anthem be, God Save The People

TWICE BLESSED

There's many a man, thats blessed with brains
Or high intelligence
But greater gifted is the man
Who's blessed with common sense

TAK' TENT

Tak' Tent is Scottish for, Take Heed, or Take Care

Enjoy your life, an' crack your joke
Tak' tent o' guid advice
Hae a dram, wi' friendly folk
It's aye nicer tae be nice

Tak' the straightest road tae steer
Whatever comes or goes
An honest stride, wi' conscience clear
Will never bruise your toes

On points of view, aye tak' your slice
But remember when ye can
Passion, Pride, and Prejudice
Are a part o' every man

Tak' tent o' a' your Kith an' Kin
For these are ties that bind
The blood is thick, the water thin
The proof, you'll always find

AN ANNUAL LOOK AT LIFE

The 'Tax-Man' has his VAT on
And life's a drudgery
We pay the price, for all things nice
Aint what it used to be

Up goes the cost of living
And more redundancy
The Unemployed, are all annoyed
Aint what it used to be

More Tax upon the petrol
The whisky, fags, and beer
But a man o' means, it always seems
Gets richer year by year

Goodbye to all our freedom
Farewell Democracy
A 'Thousand Pound', can now be found
To buy your liberty

WORTHIES O' THE ROYAL MILE

As I've said before, volumes have already been written about this Street, but this poem can apply to any street in the Country. Can you imagine the atmosphere in these streets, many, many years ago, I can only hope this poem captures some of that atmosphere.

The characters o' any street
Are aye recalled, when neighbours meet
Ower dram, or pint, or glass o' wine
Auld heids, aye mind a far off time

Back tae their faither's, faither's day
Their memories gey aften stray
When cars were jist a gyte man's dream
And horse an' cairter, reigned supreme

These cairters, and their traisty steeds
Humphed, the bulk o' city needs
Briquettes, coal, and barrelled beer
Through street, and wynd, and close, they'd steer

In mou'wart breeks, and nicky tams
These Draymen wid collect their drams
And browster wives, have made the claim
The horse aye taen the cairter hame

The hawkers, cairds, and cadgers tae
That raxt their lungs oot, every day
An' bletherin' tawpies, wid compete
A' made the Character, o' a city street

A thoroughfare, that springs tae mind
Where characters yid aye ways find
That hawked their 'gear' in leesome style
The Worthies o' the Royal Mile

Men like 'Curdy Glen' the sweep
Whae ower the sliddery roofs wid creep
'Auld Malabar', whaes jugglin' feats
Aye pulled the crowd in city streets

The 'Buckie Wife', wi' fishin' creel
Spoonin' oot her salty meal
Hawkers, wi' their pownie cairts
Displayin' fruit, fae a' the airts

'Coconut Tam', in his booler hat
Skelpin' the hand o' some theivin' brat
All chantin', as they tent their wares
Coaxin' the buyers fae their stairs

Aye The Auld Yins, aye recall this scene
And talk o' days that yince has been
They'll souk their pipes, and sup their beer
An' dream the dream, o' yester year

Fae Castlehill tae Watergate
The High Street, and Canongate
They selt their fare, wi' grace an' style
The Worthies o' the Royal Mile

SELF RESPECT

I'll show respect tae any man
On equal terms, I'll shake his hand
But tho' he hae a Title grand
I'll never grovel
I'll meet, an' speak, an' part, a Man
Of equal level

Forelock touchin', is not my game
My pride could never bear the shame
Tho' I be scant in gilt, or fame
I hae respect
I'd never desert Auld Scotia's Name
Or Dialect

A WISH

When death does come, as come it must
This Rhymer wid be thankit
Tae lie with still, posthumous pride
Beneath The Braw Blue Blanket

With this request, I'd lie at rest
Content and justified
And on the Stane, beneath my name
'Here lies a man that tried'

A STATION IN LIFE

The British Railways Board decided that the Waverley Station in Edinburgh, would now be known as Edinburgh Station.

Waverley
Braw Waverley
We're shaken tae the core
For that Southern breed
Have now decreed
Alas, your name's no more

Whae are this 'Shower'
That hae the power
Tae scythe a braw Scot's name
These faceless fiends
Now scant o' freends
Should hang their heids in shame

They plan and plot
Tae rile the Scot
Wi' a' the means at hand
They're taught at 'School'
Divide and Rule
An' you'll aye control The Land

Waverley
Proud Waverley
Born fae 'The Wizard's' brain
Guid Wattie Scott
Was known tae quote
'An Uncontaminated Name'

Guid Scots unite
And Councils fight
Tae save this proud Scot's Name
Send the message loud
Tae that 'Railway Crowd'
It's OUR HERITAGE and HAME

NEEDS

Eat according to your hunger
Drink according to your thirst
Take according to your conscience
Give according to your purse

THE HEWLITT PACKARD WA'

Dedicated to the Security Service and Members of the Hewlitt Packard Social Club, South Queensferry.

I've sipped and supped in many a club
Fae Dundee tae Macmerry
But I'll ne'er forget the Burns Nicht
They held doon at the 'Ferry

Now the 'Ferry folk are friendly folk
An' talkative an' a'
But the biggest blether that I met
Was the Hewlitt Packard Wa'

Nine inch thick, o' solid brick
An' the finest brick of course
This mortared block, could even talk
The hint legs off a horse

I've spoke tae many a Meter
Monument an' a'
But I've never met a blether
Like the Hewlitt Packard Wa'

Aye there're Lang Dykes, an' Dumbiedykes
An' Dry Stane Dykes an' a'
But they a' take second prizes
Tae the Hewlitt Packard Wa'

LINES WRITTEN ON A GET WELL CARD

Fair fa' yer honest well skelped face
We miss it sairly roon this place
It truly is a damn disgrace
That you are ailin'
And so, with First Class Post and haste
This card I'm mailin'

Never fret, you'll soon be hame
Then back tae work from whence ye came
If you leave the nurses a' alane
You'll soon recover
And save us a' much grief an' pain
Your friendly brother

SAWNEY BEAN

I was always lead to believe that cannibals were only to be found on some of the remote islands in the Tropics, seemingly this one wasn't. The Sawney Bean story, is reputed to be true, if it is, then it shows the depth of depravity, that man can sink to.

Have you heard the story
O' the Scotsman Sawney Bean
The most treacherous barbarian
This country's ever seen
He was born in fair East Lothian
When James the First was King
His faither laboured a' his life
At the hedging and the ditching

Hard work was no' for Sawney
So when he reached his teens
He ran away fae hame one day
Tae get rich by other means
And with him went a lassie
As viciously inclined
Baith suited tae each other
But two o' a different kind

They made their hame in Galloway
In a cave doon on the beach
A desolate part o' the country
Well oot o' people's reach
Nae city, town, or village
Did this pair ever see
Five an' twenty years and mair
They lived in secrecy

Sawney and his family
Fairly grew an' grew
And they in turn, had family
Quite a motley crew
They hunted like a wolf-pack
And never left a trace
Ignoring a' the wild game
They hunted members o' their race

They robbed and killed, and murdered
Without conscience, or regret
Travellers, bairns, and women
Aye, any one they met
The booty and the bodies
They'd drag back tae their lair
The treasure piled in bundles
The bodies, cut in equal share

Aye Sawney was a cannibal
And so was a' his brood
Nae contact with society
This was their only food
And a' around the district
People lived in fear
They could never find the killers
Tho' they hunted far and near

They caught and hung some innocents
They thought guilty at the time
But it didnae solve the mystery
And it didnae stop the crime
For Sawney and his cannibals
On the roads and trails wid lurk
And on unsuspecting travellers
Carried out their gory work

A couple riding hame one night
Returning from a Fair
Wound their way unknowingly
Close tae Sawney's lair
Oot jumped the Hellish Legion
Wi' Sawney in the lead
They clawed the woman tae the ground
And in seconds, she was deid

The husband drew his claymore
And began fighting for his life
Crying oot in horror
As they butchered up his wife
His cries o' help were heeded
By a party further back
And regardless o' their safety
Rode intae attack

At the sight o' these six horsemen
Sawney's clan took flight
And like ghostly apparitions
Vanished in the night

The murder was reported
Tae Glasgow Magistrate
Whae travelled tae 'Auld Reekie'
Tae see the Head o' State
When King Jamie heard their story
He gave his Royal Word
He'd hunt the 'Ghouls o' Galloway'
And put them tae the sword

The King and his Crusaders
Left the Royal grounds
Wi' four hundred fightin' soldiers
And a pack o' huntin' hounds
They scoured the County Galloway
Until they reached the beach
But nae trace o' Sawney or his tribe
Came within their reach

Then two hounds slippit fae their leads
Went howlin' on in front
The King cried out encouragement
And again took up the hunt
They found the hounds still baying
At the entrance tae a cove
Where smugglers may have stored their loot
Or pirates, their treasure trove

Wi' torches lit, they entered
Not knowing what they'd find
The putrid smell o' death around
Near drove them oot their mind
They came upon a chamber
After half a mile, at least
And there was Sawney and his clan
Engrossed, in a gory feast

Caught completely by surprise
Never thinking they'd be found
The cannibals were rounded up
Their hands and airms bound
The Crusaders then a' looked around
This Cavern o' Death
And what they saw in Sawney's lair
Made the bravest, catch their breath

For hung in rows, around the walls
Were torsoes, arms, and legs
All different shapes and sizes
Drying on their pegs
And piled against a wall
In a corner o' the cave
Lay human bones, a' picked clean
Deprived o' a decent grave

Gold and silver jewellery
Lay in piles around the flair
Swords and knives lay rusting
In the damp and salty air
The King gave his instructions
His men began their chore
The remains o' Sawney's victims
Were buried on the shore

The tribe were taen tae Glasgow
Numbering forty-eight in all
Then on tae Edinburgh City
And penned in the Tolbooth Wall
Then doon tae Leith, tae meet their fate
The cannibals were led
An eye for an eye, tooth for tooth
Was what the Guid Book said

The men were drawn and quartered
While their women stood and watched
Then they in turn, met their fate
Tied tae the stake, and torched
The tribe showed nae repentance
Not one wee bit remorse
Up tae their very last gasp o' life
They snarled, and spat, and cursed

Thus died the Sawney Bean Clan
The Ghouls o' Galloway
They'd killed hundreds, in their gory reign
Until their Judgement Day
Aye Sawney was a cannibal
Sawney was a thief
But Sawney met the Butcher
Doon at the Port o' Leith

A TENANTS REQUEST

The cowboy longed for a home, where the buffalo roamed, I'm sure it would be a lot quieter and safer, than some of the districts in Edinburgh.

Please find me a home
Where the stray dogs don't roam
Aye raikin' the buckets each day
Where the neighbours don't fight
And it's quiet every night
A place where the children can play

O find me a place
Where there's never a trace
O' mongrels, vandals, or drunks
Where the air's crystal clear
And we don't live in fear
Being mugged by some merciless punks

I'd be content wi' that hame
And never complain
And gladly pay rent when it's due
I would live out my life
Wi' my buxom wee wife
And watched a' the bairns as they grew

THE COUNCIL'S REPLY

After consulting the Council Computer, into which they have fed the facts, and after careful deliberations, comes their solution.

We've received your request
And we aye try our best
Tae satisfy everyone's needs
The question you ask
Proved quite a task
But we rose to the test, yes indeed

We've found a wee house
Just for you and your spouse
A home that is fit for a queen
Where the nights are so quiet
And there's nae sign o' riot
And the days will just pass like a dream

This place is unique
You can move in next week
And I'm sure this will prove a relief
The keys we've ENCLOSED
Of the house we've proposed
IT LIES ON THE ISLE OF INCHKEITH

THE EIGHTH WONDER O' THE WORLD

This is just to let you know, that there are sixteen Sphinxes in Edinburgh. As to how they got there, read on.

In Egypt's dry and dusty lands
No' far fae Cairo Toon
The Great Sphinx o' Gizeh stands
Or rather couches doon

This wonder o' the Ancient World
Has stood the test o' time
Survived what desert storms have hurled
And the sun's relentless shine

Now across the World, in the land o' Greece
The Female Sphinx abides
A monster o' Mythology
Withstanding time and tides

These creatures got together
Deciding tae prove their worth
And we now have Sixteen Sphinxes
In the Athens o' the North

Now the Greeks may have a word for this
And the Arabs too maybe
But of a' the Wonders in this world
It looks the Eighth tae me

There's six o' the stony creatures
Tae be found, in Parliament Square
They blend well wi' some faces
I've seen around up there

In Princes Street, just at The Mound
Eight more take their part
Round that giant mausoleum
The Academy o' Art

The North Side o' the Charlotte Square
You'll find the other two
Where the ring o' metal meters
Spoil their stony view

Tho' the climate here is different
Fae the lands from which they came
The Council aye sand-blast them a',
Tae make them feel at hame

A MONUMENTAL MYSTERY

The Walter Scott Monument, which stands in Princes Street, Edinburgh, was built in 1840-6. This magnificent structure was designed by, George Meikle Kemp, a modest carpenter, who died before seeing his work completed. In 1974 the masonry and figurines on the monument began to loosen and drop to the ground below, causing a danger to the public. The Edinburgh Town Council decided to close it and repair the damage. The structure was then enclosed in scaffolding, and repairs, which took over two years to complete, were carried out. The Architect in charge of repairs, blamed the stonemasons who had built it, seemingly, iron pins had been inserted into the bases of the figurines, instead of bronze pine. That was his story, and he's sticking to it, to find out the real story, read on.

Now there's a panic in Auld Reekie
And they don't know who tae blame
But Wattie Scott's braw monument
Will never be the same
It's been standing there quite steady
For a hundred an' thirty years
But suddenly started fallin'
Roun' Wattie's MARBLE ears

Well they gathered a' the experts
And asked them for the cause
And the answers that were given
Won them nae applause

'It seems in Queen Victoria's time'
Said one well meaning chap
'The masons nicked the bronze pins
And sold them a' for scrap
They substituted iron ones
Which rotted ower the years
And that is how the statues
Started fallin' roun' Wattie's ears'

Then up and spoke another one
Who showed some common sense
'I'm sure it was the Council
Trying tae save expense
Cutting doon on a' their cost
Jist like Scrooge the miser
Said, a pin's a pin, jist bung it in
And they'll be nane the wiser'

Well round and round they argued
Jist like a carousel
So I thought I'd play detective
And find out for masel
I daundered doon tae Princes Street
One dark and misty night
Tae try and solve the mystery
O Wattie's monumental plight

I found a fence a' round him
And a sign said 'PLEASE KEEP OUT'
The place was like a graveyard
With the statues lying about
Some covered wi' tarpaulins
Others lying face up in the night
And gazing at their stony faces
It was an eerie sight

They'd built a scaffold roon 'our man'
It was like a giant cage
And sat, among the debris
Was Wattie, white wi' rage

'How's it gaun there Wattie ?'
I shouted through a hole
'Ha, it's the man that talks tae meters'
Says Watt, 'Well bless my soul
What brings ye oot on such a night ?
There's nae parkin' meters here'
'Well I'm looking for the truth Watt
And I thought I'd find it here'

'Then crawl inside this cagework
So's nane can hear us talk
I'm fixed here kind o' permanent
And therefore cannae walk'
I crawled in through the scaffold
Where sat the mighty scholar
Wi' his wee dog Maida at his feet
Complete wi' wee dog collar

'The truth ye want, the truth ye'll get
Or as near as I can go
Sure as there's two hundred feet above me
And fifty two below'

'George Kemp was but a shepherd's lad
And a carpenter tae trade
He's the man that designed a' this
And thought his fortune made'

'He saw his work get started
And fair proud o' his creation
Two years and mair, he watched it grow
His heart burstin' wi' elation'

'But walking hame fae here one night
Fate had him on her list
He slipped an' fell in yon canal
And drowned there in the mist'

'But still his dream kept growing
Until it cleaved the sky
And I'm sure ye'll a' agree wi' me
It's gey pleasin' on the eye'

'But what about the pins', I says
Frustrated wi' masel
'I ken, I ken, I'll come tae them
So dinnae fash yersel'

'Well the Monument was finished
So elegant and tall
They thought they'd add some Statuettes
Sixty-four in all
They took them oot the books I wrote
And it was a clever plan
But may I say, I rue that day
When my troubles first began'

'They paired John Knox, wi' Charles the First
A move that proved in vain
They argued day and night until
Charlie's head came off again'

Wi' Ivanhoe, they put Rob Roy
A prankster well renowned
He'd have the shirt off a' yer backs
Or yer cattle he'd impound
'What time is it, guid Ivanhoe?'
He asked one frosty night
And the knight leaned out, tae see the clock
And vanished out o' sight'

'They are jist examples
O' what's going on up there
They're drivin' me near balmy
Man it's sair tae bear
My next door neighbour, Livingstone
They made him even wince
He turned his head away one night
And he's been like that ever since'

'But what about the pins man?'
I butted in tae say
'The pins, o' aye the bronze pins
The squirrels took them away'
'Squirrels' says I, 'Aye, squirrels' says he
'There's hundreds o' them here
It was them that nicked the bronze pins
I saw them, sitting here'

'The masons tae, they saw them
But couldnae say a word
I mean, 'Tarry Fingered' squirrels
It sounded too absurd
So they substituted iron pins
And if that lot had kept the peace
They'd have lasted a whole lot longer
Another hundred years at least'

'So somewhere in these gardens
There's a tree-load full o' scrap
And it's no' a Copper Beech tree
You can bet your life on that'

I said goodbye tae Wattie
And thanked him for the truth
I hadnae believed a word he'd said
I mean, there wasnae any proof
But every night you'll find me
Wi' a bag o' bread and cheese
An' I'm whistling at the squirrels
And tappin' at the trees

PERFECT HARMONY

Not that very long ago, one of few enjoyments in life for people, (myself included) was to go to their local pub on a Saturday night and enjoy a good 'Sing Song'. These Sing Songs were well organised by an appointed M.C. and many budding Sinatras or Perry Comos, sang their hearts out, just for the sheer pleasure of it.

Come raise your glass my merry lads
And drink a toast wi' me
A toast tae the good Auld Sing Song
And perfect harmony

Let singers sing their favourite songs
And merriment flow free
In hall or pub, in hoose or club
Wherever you may be

Let 'Dingers' dig their disco dance
Wi' lights that dirl the e'e
But gie me the Auld Time Sing Song
And perfect harmony

SPRINGTIME IN AULD REEKIE

It seems that no matter what street in Edinburgh you walk down, you will see scaffolding erected, in front of some building or other

Cauld Winter's blast, has finally past
And Spring has sprung again
Plants and shrubs are sprouting up
Despite the mist and rain

But the fastest growing Tuber
On this year's Springtime Roll
Is the leafless, flowerless, shapeless stalk
the silver scaffold pole

It climbs the walls like ivy
In straight and parallel shoots
It can even grow on concrete
For this tuber has no roots

It has changed the 'Face' o' Reekie
This Silver Stalagmite
Where once grand stately buildings stood
Steel cages fill the site

Aye, Springtime in Auld Reekie
Once the 'Athens of the North'
Doesn't seem the same today
It's now the 'Steel Town by the Forth'

THE FLOWER O' PRESTONFIELD

This poem refers to my Mother-in-Law Minnie Reilly, a Southsider who died in 1976, the four seeds referred to, are one son, and three daughters. There is no flower called the Einnim, the word is Minnie spelt backwards.

There was a flower in Prestonfield
That blossomed every year
She was a hardy annual
A small and bonnie dear

They called this flower the Einnim
And four seeds did she yield
These seeds now have taken root
From the Flower o' Prestonfield

But in the Spring o' Seventy-Six
The Gardener, took his walk
He raised Time's Deadly Sickle
And cut through her slender stalk

No more will the bonnie Einnim bloom
Her roots are now a' sealed
No other flower can take her place
The Flower o' Prestonfield

A MAN IN HIBERNATION

The winter of 1978-79, was a long one in more ways than one, many people suffered needlessly through strikes, etc., road were impassable, pavements impossible to walk on. It was also Election Year, and the Politicians were making their usual promises, and I thought, how nice it would be, if a man, like some of the animals, could just curl up and go to sleep in the winter, and let it all blow over.

O wake me when this winter's over
Wake me when the snow has gone
Shake me when the ice has melted
And when the roads are dry as bone

Call me when the strikes have ended
When everyone have their per-cent
When all their differences are mended
Call me when they're all content

Rouse me when Election's over
Just in case I've overslept
When all the promises and pledges
Shake me when they've all been kept

Awakened now, and feeling rested
None the worse for wear or tear
Nothing's changed, as I expected
They've let me sleep for owre a year

A PATRIOT'S ADDRESS

Like every Scotsman, I am 'chuffed' to see Scotland qualify for the World Cup, and caught up in the fever that has spread throughout the Country, I thought this is how I would (if I could) address the Scottish Team, and most of all the great Scottish Support, before the 'battle' of the World Cup in Argentina.

Scots whae Willie Ormond formed
Scots whae through the turnstiles stormed
Scots wi' Tartan a' adorned
Shout for Victory

Now's the time and now's the hour
Show your still a fitba power
Let them see the Scottish Flower
Play for Victory

Whae can match the Scottish Fans
Fae John o' Groats tae the Border lands
Follow, follow, clap your hands
Gie them Victory

Hear them chant 'McLeod, McLeod'
Ally's Army's done us proud
Sing 'The Flower' and sing it loud
The Song of Victory

Whae for Scotland's Team an' a'
Widnae kick that leathered ba'
Whae wid say we'll lose or draw
Let him turn and flee

Play until your legs are numb
Sing until your a' struck dumb
Argentina, here we come
Bound for Victory

When you reach that foreign shore
Let the Lion Rampant roar
Burst your lungs when Scotland score
And we'll hae Victory.

THE BREATHELYSER

The message, I think is obvious, 'Don't drink and Drive'.

I went tae a Burns Supper
Just the other night
I packed masel wi' haggis
And ended up, quite tight

I said goodnight tae everyone
My how the time had flown
I stepped outside the door tae find
A howlin' gale was blowin'

My head bent down against the wind
The road gey wet an' greasy
Intae the car, start it up
Now Davy, take it easy

I'll keep tae a' the quiet roads
My God, it's bloody dark
I'll cut doon by the Palace
And up roon through the park

Up past the Halls o' Residence
Turn left there, at the Pool
I'm on the Dalkeith Road now
And tryin' tae keep ma cool

But what's that there in front o' me
A Police sign saying 'SLOW'
I draw intae the left-hand kerb
There's nae where else tae go

The Deil himsel', is standing there
Wi' three stripes, on his arm
Come on Davy, think man
Use yer wit and charm

He opened up the car door
My feet were lumps o' lead
His nostrils flared, twice, in an' oot
And then, he shook, his head

'We've had a little bevvy sir'
And he gave his mate a nudge
I says, 'Yer lucky Mr. Polisman
I'm sober as a judge'

'Blow inside this baggie sir
Don't give us any fuss'
It was then I started thinkin'
Oh, I wish I'd got the bus

But I blew inside his baggie
And never let it sag
And two wee horns, started growin'
Oot the bottom o' the bag

The Sergeant's mouth hung open
As he watched the wee horns grow
'I'm sorry sir, here try this one'
Again, I began tae blow

But again the same thing happened
And the Sergeant's face was white
He turned around, tae seek advice
But his mate, was oot o' sight

'Tell me, what have you been drinking
For the bags tae act sae queer?'
'Bovril', was my quick reply
And he bawled, 'Get out o' here'

So if yer prone tae drinking
Make it 'Bovril' or Beef Tea
For 'I'll never forget, the two wee horns
And what they did for me.

THE WILTED FLOWER

The World Cup in Argentina was, for Scotland, an embarrassment, a debaucle, a disappointment, especially to those fans that had travelled to Argentina to witness it. It was also a big let-down to all the wee laddies who were wearing the Scottish shirts, badges, hats, etc., that were on sale at that time, and who actually believed Scotland could win the World Cup. Even though we beat Holland in the last game, the damage had been done.

Scots whae believed in Ally's con'
Scots whae froze on the Cordoba lawn
Scots whae Peru left all forlorn
Ye brought pain and misery

Whae'd have thought the Scottish Flower
Wid be trampled doon amang the stour
Instead o' Scotland's finest hour
Came shame and misery

When on tae meet Iran, they went
But again, came off wi' heids a' bent
Scottish pride, took another dent
They played disgracefully

What happened tae the fire and zest
That beats in every Scotsman's breast
That's turned the tide, when e'er oppressed
Missing on that day

Fae the Scottish Fans, that crossed the sea
Tae the millions watching on T.V.
Everyone, will aye agree
Ye shamed the Scottish Jersey

Ally spouts, he's not tae blame
Scoring goals, is the name o' the game
What hurts most, midst a' the shame
They scored commercially

You that bear the name o' Scot
What cancerous image hae ye wrought
If you had only tried, and fought
And gave us hope that day

What happens now, only time will tell
We'll build again, fae an empty shell
But it seems, we'll always beat oursel'
It's in our History.

WHO WERE THE SCOTS

Professor Ian Grimble, a Scottish Historian, had a Series on Television called, 'Who Were The Scots'. In this programme he traced back to the very first Inhabitants of Scotland, there were six serials in the programme, and the last one left me feeling (with no offence to Mr. Grimble) that maybe he had left out the most important Scots.

Mr. Ian Grimble, you gave us quite a shock
By inquiring on the Telly
Who were the famous Scots
The men I'd like tae talk about
Were Great and Worthy Scots
And deserve a wee bit mention
When you're on that Goggle-Box

Auld Scotland's bred some heroes bold
And o' their deeds tales have been told
Men like Douglas, Stewart, and Bruce
Whae sometimes fought, or signed a truce
All heroes great, yet none could fill
The socks or boots o' 'Guardian Wull'
The greatest Scotsman, ever born
A fighter worthy o' his corn

Inventions next, and we've had a few
It's amazing what the Scots can do
Logie-Baird gave us our Tellies
Dunlop gave us Tyres and Wellies
Macadam smoothed off a' our roads
By spreadin' Tar, in Barry-loads
Guid Simpson's sleepy Chloroform
Helped the surgeons a' perform
Fleming's Penicillin injection
Cleared your wounds o' a' infection
Steam Engines, Radar, and I'll bet
That Scotsmen, arnae finished yet

Writers next, we're among the best
Their works have stood both time an' test
Sir Walter Scott, gave us Ivanhoe
And Scottish Tales, o' long ago
R.L. Stevenson, ye mind wi' pride
Gave us 'Kidnapped', Jekyll an' Hyde
An' I'm sure ye a' remember fine
Buchan's 'Steps o' Thirty Nine'

James Barrie's tale o' 'Peter Pan'
Wid melt the heart o' any man
Tho' a' were great, each in their turns
The greatest one of a', was Burns
His works are known in every Lan'
Fae Timbuctoo tae Yucatan
And Scotsmen still are gaining fame
Wi' men like Tranter and MacLean
There's mair will come, I'd even bet
Aye Scotsmen arnae finished yet

In the Sporting World, we've made our mark
Wi' Jacky Stewart and Jimmy Clark
Buchanan, Lynch, an' Wee McGowan
Proved the Scots were overpowrin'
And Scots that gave us sheer delight
Slim Jim, The Lawman, and John White
Their skills aye gave us a' a treat
the men wi' magic in their feet

We invented golf, and tatties crispy
Haggis, porridge oats, an' whisky
Bannocks, broth, and other food
They even say our Special's good
Sherlock Holmes, an' Burke an' Hare
Tam o' Shanter, and his mare
Highlanders, Lowlanders, Borderers, an' a'
East Coast, West Coast, Scotsmen one an' a'

Tae this wee Rugged Country
The world is in our debt
An' I say again that Scotsmen
Arnae finished yet

WINTER

Slowly
With unrelenting advance
Comes the grip of Winter

The mornings
Of sparkling crystallized dew
Hardening, into layers of unshiftable ice
Softened only
By the falls of feathered snowflakes
Covering the Earth
In a blanket of blinding whiteness

'NATIONAL' HEALTH OR SICKNESS

There's Scots wha hae, and Scots wha don't
There's Scot wha will, and Scots wha won't
There's Scots wi' far mair than their share
Will scheme around for mair an' mair
Once siller's caught in their greedy mitts
They'd round the corners on Ten-Bob-Bits

There's ither Scots that maim an' kill
Muggers, villains, the jails are full
Tho' Scottish Law deals wi' their crimes
Alas, too leniently at times

There's ither Scots, when it came tae vote
Showed mair colours than Jacob's coat
In 'Auld Lang Syne' tae their Country's shame
When battles raged, they stayed at hame
In 'Parliament Hall' ye'll mind that date
They left this Country tae it's fate
In 'Union' these political lice
Sold this Nation for a price

But the worst Scot, in this Land aroun'
Is the one that runs Auld Scotia doon
Nae words describe this treacherous Scot
For he's the one that starts the rot
Curses on his blackened soul
May he roast in that fiery hole

O wid some Power, the gift tae gie us
And fae these parasites, a' free us
And that same Power, destroy the 'Lease'
That has sold this Country, piece by piece
Then, wi' every Scotsman tae his station
We'd be a proud and worthy Nation

LIMERICK

There was a young man from Dunoon
Who blew up a big red balloon
As he loosened his grip
It stuck to his lip
He was found on a tree-top in Troon.

THE MONARCH O' THE MOZZIES

Of a' the beasties in this world
That bite an' claw, and scratch
There's one that rates abin them a'
The rest can never match

The terror o' the tourist
He'll make them squirm an' fidge
The Piranha o' the peat bogs
The wee West Highland Midge
This carniverous wee creature
Makes the bravest men turn pale
Has them clawin' an' a-slappin'
A' tae nae avail

They cover thersel's in lotions
Use sprays an' creams tae match
But the wee West Highland Midgie
Aye brings them up tae scratch

So cover up yer bodies
No matter where ye gaun
For the Monarch o' the Mozzies
Might be lurkin' near at haun

A NEW YEAR'S DAWN

1979 has come and gone, the Year of the Child they called it, a year full of strikes, poverty, starvation, refugees etc.

The New Year's Day, has finally dawned
Hogmanay has come and gone
Auld Father Time, resets his clock
His grey auld heid, again takes stock

He turns ahint, his eyes fu' glassed
Tae ponder ower the Year that's passed
A Year he doubled checked, and filed
Ironically 'The Year o' Child'

Hate and hunger, reigned supreme
Peace and plenty, still a dream
A Year o' shame, he now reflects
And unrepentin' Man forgets

He lifts his scythe, and cuts it free
To drift in the Realms o' History
Then turns the glass, wi' tender care
And lets the sand flow on once mair

OLD TOMMY

'Tommy' is a sculpture in fibre glass, by Malcolm Robertson, set in a Sculpture Park in the Glenshee area. The Park was opened in 1975, and all the Exhibits are mainly abstract. 'Tommy' was modelled on a resident in an old folks home, in the West of Scotland. The Sculpture was originally in a Glasgow Gallery.

He sits there alone, in his mountain retreat
The fibre glass man, on his fibre glass seat
Unaware o' the wind, the rain, or the sleet
The silent guard o' Glenshee

Nae soul has Auld Tam, for the world tae infest
Nae brain in his heid, nae heart in his breast
But he sits there in comfort, as Auld Nature's guest
Enjoying the view o' Glenshee

Tho' his unseeing eyes, never witness the dawn
Nor his stationary feet, tread Nature's Lawn
He'll still be there, when we have all gone
The Fibre Glass Man o' Glenshee

THE MARTIAN SUPPER

This is the story of 'Brief Encounters of a Different Kind'. In the winter of 1978-79, U.F.O.'s were sighted all around Scotland the Martians were coming, the reason being, that, as we hold our Annual 'Burns Supper' every year, so the Martians hold their annual 'Martian Supper'. They always invite (or kidnap) an Earthman as their 'Guest' of honour, and that year it happened to be me.

I'm no' a man tae cause a fuss
Or look for any bother
I take my dram, I swear and curse
Just like any other
An average man you might well say
Intelligent, but humble
I smile when things are going right
But when they're wrong, I grumble

I'll tell the truth, when asked for it
But may I say take heed
For with steady eye, I'd tell a lie
If I thought there was a need
With truth in mind, and steady eye
This tale tae you I'll tell
And whether you believe it
Well, that's up tae you yersel

It happened late one winter's night
Owre by the Castlebrae
Again I cursed the 'Gritter's Strike'
For making me come that way
My head bent doon against the wind
I trudged on through the snow
The Castle Ruins now in sight
I stopped tae have a blaw

Then gatherin' strength tae carry on
I suddenly became aware
O' a strange pulsating rhythm
Fillin' the cauld night air
Nae earthly music this I thought
Yet pleasant tae my ear
It seem tae pass right through me
Dispellin' doubt and fear

My eyes trained on the Castle Walls
Trying tae find the source
I felt masel, drawn tae it's doors
By a strange compellin' force
From the shadows, came a voice
And bid me, step inside
But being of sound an' cautious mind
I stood quite firm, outside

A moment passed, I found my voice
And asked the unseen face
'Your voice seems very friendly, man
But is there nae lights in this place
The voice then gave a sharp command
The music began tae grow
And oot fae the Hawkill Wood, it came
A GIANT U.F.O.

It hummed it's way owre passed us
Then, a momentary pause
And slowly, finally, settled doon
On the roofless, Castle wa's
It's under-carriage lights beamed on
Flooding the place wi' light
I stood there rooted tae the spot
At the strange, unearthly sight

Within it's doors, I saw a hall
Wi' tables a' in line
And around them sat a multitude
Waiting there tae dine
I was ushered gently forward
And they a' rose tae their feet
And there in a place of honour
They offered me a seat

They all sat down, excepting one
The Spokesman, for that night
'A thousand welcomes earthman
Tae our 'Martian Supper Night''
Have no fear the speaker said
Our aim is tae impress
And in true traditional fashion
We'll begin with 'The Address'

A giant pie, on a silver tray
Was transported shoulder high
And placed before the Speaker
Who thus addressed the pie

ADDRESS TAE THE PIE

Italians drool owre Minestrone
Bolognaise and Macaroni
Sassenachs have raised their brood
On roasted beef and Yorkshire Pud
The French prefer the frog and snail
Then down the vino by the pail
On T-boned steaks, the Yanks will swear
Barbecued or medium rare

The Paddies love their Irish Stew
Followed by their local brew
The Russki favours Caviar
Then downs the Vodka by the jar
The Jocks, a proud an worthy race
Whae'd meet the Devil face tae face
Will fill their plates in tidy heaps
Wi' Haggis, Tatties, and Champit Neeps

But take a Martian fae the skies
Point him where Auld Scotland lies
He has one thought, and that's his prize
Oxo cubes, and hot mince pies
Ye powers that made the planet Mars
Out o' crusty pies and bovril jars
The cheesy moons, and custard suns
Bless us, hungry Martians

Trays o' pies were piled in heaps
On each and every table
And the Martians started muckin' in
As fast as they were able
Pots o' steaming Bovril
Were ladled out in jugs
And tae the cries o' 'Cheers, Ah Bisto'
The Martians raised their mugs

At last the meal was finished
And midst the burps and sighs
I asked tae hear the story
O' the travellers fae the skies

'Well the Martian's a pie-coholic
He'll wolf any kind o' pie
Be it mince, steak, or kidney
Baked, steamed, or fried
And he loves the taste o' Bovril
He'll sing on jist one sip
And whae the hell can blame him
Wi' whisky, forty pence a nip'

'You might think this winter murder
But it's a blessing in disguise
Wi' the fitba' a' bein' cancelled
There was a stockpile o' mince pies
We were seen a' roon the country
People spotted our U.F.O.
For where there's pies, our future lies
And a Martian has tae go'

'And go we must now Earthman
I hope you've enjoyed your night'
Then I was gently ushered out
By the leader o' the flight
The music started up again
And the U.F.O. took flight
Then disappeared in the cauld night sky
As fast as the speed o' light

I found masel alone again
Trudgin' through the snow
Thinkin' o' the Martians
And their giant U.F.O.
Nae gritter's strike tae worry them
The gourmets o' the skies
As around they go, in their U.F.O.
In their endless search for pies

But mortal man, draws a different plan
Has a different kind o' greed
Are we the alien race, in an alien place
Born of an alien seed
So if you ever meet a Martian
Or see a U.F.O. at night
Remember the Martian Supper
And pie-coholic flight

THE HANDYMAN

Some men are very handy around the house, and some of course aren't

Spare a thought for the good old Handyman
And always wish him well
A 'Jack of all the Trades' man
And Master o' himsel'

What wid we dae without him
He's always there on call
He'll fix a fuse, or mend a leak
Or plaster up a wall

He'll cut the hedge, or fix the fence
Or oil a squeaking door
He'll plant an' sow, prune and mow
And handle any chore

Yet maist wives keep complaining
Their backs are always sore
For they maintain the Handyman
Always lives next door

WORDS

A few simple words which, I hope, explains what a friend really is, as the word is used far too loosely at times.

Of all the words, that e'er were printed
Such as honesty, truth, and good
I'd choose a word, that's oftened used
But so often, misunderstood
The meaning of the word is plain
To be it, can be called humane
To find it, sometimes proves in vain
Still, we keep searching
Until one day, it's standing there
Ready and waiting

Tho' worth it's weight in solid gold
This printed Eldorado
Money cannot buy it, nor any false bravado
It's value lies within the heart
Or at a rainbow's end
The word is very simple, man
The word in fact, is FRIEND

AN IMMORTAL MEMORY

Many volumes have been written and published, by many famous people, concerning Scotland's National Bard, Robert Burns, this is just a simple, modest rhyme, which is not meant to compete with the famous works already mentioned, (not that it would) but if it ever encourages anyone after reading it, to become interested in Burns, then that would indeed be a compliment. His songs and poems are world famous, yet not enough of his life and works, are taught in our schools.

In Seventeen Hundred and Fifty-Nine
In a place called Alloway
Robert Burns the poet was born
On January's Twenty-Fifth day

But before I talk aboot oor Rab
And that's clearly my intention
I'll say a word aboot his folk
For they're worthy o' a mention

His faither's name was Wull Burness
From the Shire o' Kincardine
A farmer's son, a worthy man
Whae shouldered life's hard burden

His parents having struck hard times
Wull and his brother Bob
Decided they wid leave the hoose
And go searching for a job

They baith shook hands, an' went their ways
Each vowing tae take care
And Wull came South tae Edinburgh
Tae seek his fortune there

He worked as a gardener in the Toon
But couldnae settle there
So he made his way South Westward
Tae the bonnie toon o' Ayr

He worked for the Laird o' Fairly
And mair than proved his worth
Until one day, he took a lease
On his ain wee bit o' earth

He built a sma' 'Clay-biggin''
No' far fae Alloway Kirk
Then decided he'd get married
Just tae finish off his work

He met and courted Agnes Broun
And in wedlock they were sworn
And in their humble dwelling
The Poet Rab was born

Nature welcomed in oor Rab
Wi' a gale o' ragin' force
It blew the cottage wa' doon
As it howled past on it's course

Schooling was essential
As Rabbie stretched an' grew
His faither and young Murdoch
Taught him a' they knew

Another thing he learnt
Amidst the toil an' strife
Was a first hand education
In the University o' life

The family moved tae Oliphant
Then on tae farm Lochlea
But hard times kept on doggin' them
And widnae let them be

But through these times o' drudgery
The Genius started showing
He put tae verse, the things he saw
While ploughin' or a-mowing

The Mouse, the Lark, the Wounded Hare
Were thankful for his pen
The Auld Mare, Thrush, and Daisy
He immortalised a' them

But that pen became a weapon
Against snobbery and deceit
Against meanness and oppression
And cruelty and conceit

Oor Rab was patriotic
And loved Auld Scotland dear
He brought Her Songs tae life again
And tae many an eye, a tear

Whae can forget his 'Scots Wha Hae'
Freedom's Battle Hymn
It stirs the blood in every Scot
Near fit tae burst their skin

Or the World's National Anthem
The famous 'Auld Lang Syne'
This friendly song, will aye be sung
Until the end of time

But in every man, there is a flaw
And Rab was nae exception
There's many whae have missed a rung
On the ladder of perfection

Ye see, Rabbie loved the lassies
Since he was in his teens
And the lassies loved oor Rabbie
For he treated them like Queens

But in a' these passionate escapades
There was only one love in his life
And that was bonnie Jean Armour
His understanding wife

Twas Jean, that shared his heartbreaks
When Nature wid deprive
She gave birth tae his nine children
And only three survived

Throughout their grief and sorrow
Nae rosy picture could they paint
And if Rab was e'er a sinner
Then Jean Armour was a saint

Rab composed the sweetest love songs
Songs which the world still sing
'Ae Fond Kiss', and 'Red Red Rose'
And tender 'Bonnie Wee Thing'

But of a' the songs he e'er composed
The most popular it would seem
Was 'Of A' The Airts The Wind Can Blaw'
Which he pledged tae his Bonnie Jean

Rab laughed at life's misfortunes
And tried tae live life tae it's full
But life was like an ocean
And Rab a wee bit pool

But what a Pool o' Genius
Oor Rabbie proved tae be
An honest, working farmer's boy
Brimful o' poetry

The Chinese claim him as their ain
The Russians, as a brother
Ye can search the Books o' Literature
And ye'll never find another

The World will aye be in his debt
Which ever way it turns
For the Poems and Songs will never die
O' Immortal Rabbie Burns

In Seventeen Hundred and Ninety-Six
Alas it came tae pass
That on July the Twenty-First
Oor Rabbie breathed his last
Tonight we Toast his Memory
On this conspicuous date
To a Patriot and a Ploughman
Auld Scotland's 'Poet Laureate'

THE FORTH RANGER

The Forth Ranger, is a launch based at Granton Harbour, with a crew of four, of which my brother Frank is one. Being well equipped, it checks the pollution levels in the Firth of Forth.

Whae keeps the Firth o' Forth sae clean
Asked the total stranger
I'll tell ye whae, says I wi' pride
The crew o' the auld Forth Ranger

Whae checks pollution on the Forth
Tae save the fish fae danger
The Captain and his triple crew
In the launch they call Forth Ranger

So here's a toast, tae ship and crew
I'll vow they'll never change her
O what I'd gie, tae put tae sea
For a trip on the auld Forth Ranger

BURNS SUPPERS

When Nor' West winds blaw icy past
And skies are black and overcast
When hail an' snaw aye swirl an' blast
And days are dreich
Another 'Supper' breaks ma fast
The fourth this week

Wi' driftin' snaw piled up in banks
Ma thermal drawers wrapt roon ma shanks
I jine the ever growing ranks
Tae sing Rab's praise
I gie 'The Bard' ma heartfelt thanks
For happy days

Wi' Tam o' Shanter in ma brain
And Holy Willie doon the drain
I take ma leave and daunder hame
Aye takin' tent
Trouble an' care, leave me alane
This man's content

But wid some power that's lookin' doon
Change Burns's birthday tae sunny June
All Scotia's lads wid sing in tune
Wi' worthy cause
They'd toss their thermals tae the moon
In loud applause

THE KONKERED DUKE

I've always called a chestnut a 'konker', as every laddie who ever played the game did, hence the title. The story about the farmer and his laddie, is reputed to be true, the Duke, and his horse of course don't talk, or do they?

There's a statue in Aul' Reekie
Across fae the G.P.O.
People pass it every day
Going to and fro
The statue is o' Wellington
The man o' Waterloo
The Duke that beat Napoleon
An' pulled Europe oot a stew

His real name's Arthur Wellesley
And in Dublin, lay his roots
He's the first o' the Irishmen
Tae wear the 'Welly Boots'
He sits there royally on his horse
Looking brave an' braw
Aye the statue's gey impressive
But the statue has a flaw

Tae find out mair about it
I took my usual walk
And went down tae view the statue
Tae see if the Duke would talk

'Good evening tae your Lordship
Or should I say Your Grace
It's a privilege and a pleasure
Tae meet ye face tae face
You've quite a reputation
Since that day at Waterloo
When ye beat that wee French 'Upstart'
And gave him what was due'

'Ah, good evening tae you, Scotsman
Or should I call you Jock
I've heard a bit, about you tae
Fae my neighbour Watt Scott
But what brings ye doon tae see me
There's nothing happening here'
'Well, I'm doon tae look ye over
For there is a flaw, I hear'

'A flaw', he shouted angrily
'I'm afraid you've went too far
Napoleon thought the same, man
That's how he lost the war'

'Now calm yersel', your Lordship
There's nae flaws on you, of course
If ye had've let me finish
The flaw is on your horse
Ye see, your horsey has nae chestnuts
I KNOW, they grow on trees
But these are the 'corns' or hard lumps
Behind a horse's knees'

'Well, I've been sitting on this 'cuddy's' back
Since Eighteen Fifty Two
And I must admit, in a' that time
That's a thing I never knew
It could've been that winter
Wi' a' the ice and snaw
It happens tae brass monkeys
It could happen tae a horse an a''

Now the horse, that had been quiet 'til now
Suddenly came awake
It landed doon on a' it's fours
And gave itsel' a shake
'Pardon me for interruptin'
But if ye want tae know the truth
Where else could ye get it
Except straight from the horse's mooth'

'There's three metals on this statue
But only one is real
There's the Iron Duke, the statue's Bronze
And it was built by a man named Steele
And when John Steele had finished it
He thought 'man, that looks braw
I'll gie ten pounds, tae anyone
If they can find a flaw''

'Now a farmer and his laddie
In the Toon tae look around
Were marvelling at the Monuments
And at every sight and sound
The laddie fairly loupin' roun'
Draggin' his faither's hand
'Dad see this', an' 'look at that'
And 'Dad', 'is that no' grand''

'Well, they came up tae our statue
And looked us owre gey close
They'd heard about Sir John Steele
And his equally famous boast
The laddie grabbed his faither's arm
Aye tryin' hard tae please
'I think I've found the flaw dad
There's nae lumps at the horse's knees'

'Ye're right enough there laddie'
Showing his son respect
'Come on now, dinnae hing aboot
We'll find the architect'
They found John Steele, whae was mair than pleased
At what the lad had found
And he put the boy through college
In place o' the ten pound

Says I, 'That was a rare wee story
Have ye anything else tae say'
The horse reared up on it's baith hint legs
And answered, 'Neigh, neigh, neigh'
So now you know the story
O' the statue wi' the flaw
But stand direct in front o' it
And man, it still looks braw

TRIBUTE TO A FRIEND

The following lines are dedicated to my good friend and brother-in-law, the late John Fisher.

Farewell good friend, a last and fond farewell
The 'Ferryman' stands impatient at the pier
Sounding out his lone and deathly knell
The time of parting, is already here

Goodbye, goodbye, the final words are muted
Set sail on your voyage from this shore
The ties with us mortals, now uprooted
Your memory, will linger evermore

With bursting heart, and tear-filled eyes, I swallow
The pains of sorrow, burning me inside
All I ask, on the day when I must follow
Is your courage, dignity, and pride

No more the 'Ballad Songs' of 'Como'
Or 'Love is All', your favourite sweet refrain
These melodies will always be remembered
For you may never pass this way again

NICKNAMES

Nicknames are part and parcel of every day life in the shipyards, on the rigs, and on building sites, etc., below are just a few.

There was Sober Sam the Plumber
Weel kent in every pub
An' Dick the Dark Destroyer
Aye lookin' for a sub

A tarry fingered magpie
Whae hailed fae Tiger Bay
They called him the Taiwan Tea-Leaf
Or the Chinky Take-Away

There was Injun Joe a Navahoe
An' a chieftan o' his breed
A Sikh, aye on the panel
They called him Sair's-Maheid

A welder, name o' Wing Nut
His ears stood oot his heid
And a blue eyed bloke called Tumshie
Because he was a Swede

There was Tick, whae lent you money
When things were very slack
And if your slow in payments
Tock, aye got it back

A sour faced Gaffer Joiner
They called him Rent-a-smile
And Desperate Dan the Hardman
Who was never oot the Jile

A Caulker, named The Sprinter
Because the man could shift
And a rigger, named The Hiker
Aye lookin' for a lift

There will always be a nickname
When you work among a crew
And how you earn the honour
Is entirely up to you

HOW FAR HAVE WE COME

How far have we come
In this world of civilised Christianity
When, confronted with depression, we turn away
Only to meet, the snarling face of aggression
Again we turn, take another direction
With eyes seeking, searching, probing
For just a glimpse of hopeful intention
Only to be blinded, by the threat of Nuclear Expulsion

How far have we come
When, hunger, disease, and malnutrition
Are the constant companions, of the less fortunate
Their only crime being, their geographic position
Born, only to die, defrauded of life, and deserted
By the unscrupulous laws, of ambitious leaders
While lying among the ruins of history
Are the discarded Laws of Common Humanity

How far have we come
When, fear and suspicion, greed and power
Profit and gain, are allowed to flower, unhindered
And in the drugged sleep of apathy
We dream the impossible dream
In a world full of jealousy and hate
It seems, as Human Beings
We have not come far

EPITAPH

All alone, beneath this stone
Lies a cowan, name o' Knight
He lived and died in darkness
Having never saw the light

DEATH

O cowardly Death, whae stills the breath
And brings Life tae an end
When striking honest mortals
Why must it be a friend

HOME SERVICE FORCE

The Home Service Force, (H.S.F.) which was formed in 1985, is an updated equivalent of the old Home Guard, and ex-soldiers were asked to volunteer.

Three cheers for 'Auld Dad's Army'
The gallant H.S.F.
Tho' half o' them are cripples
And the other half are deaf

Fae farms and towns and seaside ports
By bribery or wage
They gethered men o' a' the sorts
Regardless o' their age

This merry Geriatric Force
Unwrapped their bows and spears
And volunteered their services
Plus blood and sweat and tears

But now they guard Auld Scotia's shores
Wi' bayonet, pride and gun
They're aye alert, they'll ne'er desert
Cause they're jist too auld tae run

Of all the world's great Regiments
Who've fought throughout the years
They can't compare, with the debonair
Hot Shot Fusiliers

TRAFFIC WARDEN'S SONG

I know of no other group of workers more dedicated to their work, than the Traffic Wardens in Edinburgh.

In our black and yellow suits
And our Doctor Marten boots
We patrol around the streets all day
And if your parking free
Then we do our dance of glee
And through the nose you'll always have to pay

We are a special breed
And we're ruthless, yes indeed
Our emblem is the Heart of Stone
We hate your smiling face
It's an absolute disgrace
We always love to hear you wail and moan

Now we're maybe no' that bright
But when we come in sight
The cars will always disappear from view
You'll maybe get away
But we'll catch you some sweet day
And leave a little present there for you

We've a Sergeant in our 'Pen'
Who's a credit to his men
In education, he never won a star
His favourite colour's pink
And he always likes to think
That a touch of it's displayed on every car

We will catch you unaware
By hiding in a stair
Or peeking round a corner out of view
And when you think the coast is clear
That's when we appear
And another sucker's landed in the stew

You can call us what you want
But you'll never ever daunt
Our proud and concientious 'Corps'
We're that thick behind the ears
And immune to all your tears
For we've heard your hard luck stories all before

Aye in our black and yellow suits
And our 'Docky Marten' boots
We'll follow that long and yellow line
Until the streets become quite bare
With no one parking there
Then we'll look around for someone else to fine.

ETHIOPIA 1984

What is this road, that some must tread
Paved with Misery and Dread
Where the Needs of Life, are thinly spread
Tae their last breath
The Balance, hanging by a Thread
From Birth tae Death

This Ragged Mass, of Skin and Bone
Who trudge this Barren Road alone
Their dreams of Life and Hope are gone
They only Mime
Tenants of a Torrid Zone
Their only Crime.

REMORSE

I always like to think that every Scotsman has a conscience, and this being so, I'm sure that this is how 'Bonnie Prince Charlie' must have felt about Culloden, and also what happened afterwards.

Cauld as the blast that blaws in fae the Hebrides
Bare as the pebbles on Scotia's grey shore
Such is the welcome, that always will wait for me
After That Day, on thon Blood-Soakit Moor

Braw were the Lads that laid down their lives for me
Crushed by Cumberland's butcherous power
Scribes will record, their stout hearted bravery
Had I died with them, on Culloden's Grey Moor

Had I charged with them against the Artillery
Or fell with the bravest, amangst a' the glaur
Or even returned, to share in their misery
I left them to die, on that Blood-Soakit Moor.

NATURE'S WAY

What's that mist coming off the ground
O what's that mist my Daddie
That's nae mist, but Nature's breath
It's just the Earth a-breathing laddie

O what's this rain that's falling fast
That soaks us tae the skin my Daddie
That's no' rain, but once again
It's just the Angels crying laddie

What makes the leaves a' turn tae brown
And fall off a' the trees my Daddie
It's Nature shedding her Golden Crown
They'll bloom again in Springtime laddie

What makes the sun tae shine sae bright
And turn the day sae warm my Daddie
It means that Summer's come in sight
It's just the Heavens smiling laddie.

JESSIE'S MICRO-WAVE

This is what happened when one poor woman tried to cook an old fashioned recipe, in a new-fangled machine.

Our Jessie was a houseproud wife
Whae kept her kitchen braw
And a' the modern gear in life
Stood along the wa'
An' sitting on a worktop
Was the pride an' joy o' Jess
An oven o' proportions
A Micro-Wave no less

This computerised wee cooker
A labour saving dream
Could tenderise the toughest meat
Wi' never a trace o' steam
It's dashboard full o' dials
It did everything but sing
And ye'd need a Pilot's licence
Jist tae work the bloody thing

Came the day o' 'Rabbie's' Birthday
And our Jessy played her card
'We'll hae a Burns Supper
Jist tae celebrate the Bard'
So she gethered a' the family
An' gave them a' a chore
Then grabbin' her hat an' handbag
She rushed oot through the door

Doon tae the local butcher's shop
At a fast and furious gait
An' bought herself ae 'Haggis'
That wid grace a 'Royal Plate'
Then scampering back tae her braw wee kitchen
All systems now at 'Go'
But alas unknown tae Jessy
We come tae our tale o' woe

While the soup was simmering
Jessy committed a crime
She stuffed the haggis in the Micro-Wave
Tae save hersel' some time
As they supped their 'Cockaleekie'
Savouring the country tang
From the precincts o' the kitchen
There came an almighty 'BANG'

They a' sat there dumfoonered
Then rose tae their feet as one
And hurried tae the kitchen
Tae see what damage had been done

Well, there wis haggis on the ceiling
Haggis ower the floor
Haggis on the windaes
An' haggis on the door
The oven door wis open
And hinging on one hinge
And what was once her pride an' joy
Now made Jessy cringe

As they a' jist stood there staring
The Computer began tae 'Tick'
An' a wee white flag, rose oot the top
Tied tae a wee white stick
The Micro-Wave surrendered
Then collapsed in a smokin' heap
And the guiding light o' Jessy's life
Was reduced now tae a peep

But our Jessy's learn't her lesson now
Fae that eventful day
That the best laid plans o' women
Sometimes gang astray
So sure as water, blends wi' whisky
An' malt is taken neat
Wi' Micro-Chips an' Haggis
Never the Twain should meet.

THE POSTPONMENT

On the 10th of March, 1982, some learned people predicted that the World would end, it didn't happen, and no reasons were given. The answer is given below.

God and Auld Man Moses
Sat talking on a cloud
Said God tae Auld Man Moses
Jist look doon at that crowd

Pointin' his finger Earthwards
Covering everyone in sight
I think the time has come Mo'
Tae gie that lot a fright

What aboot a flood Mo'
I'll open up the skies
It widnae dae much harm Lord
They've got ships o' giant size

Well I'll send Hell-fire and Brimstone
And that should fix them Mo'
They've Anti-Nuclear Shelters Lord
That's where they a' wid go

Then I'll plague the world wi' Locusts Mo'
Like I did in Days of Yore
Sorry Lord, their D.D.T.
Kills them by the score

Aye they're crafty folk, these Humans Mo'
They've learnt their lessons well
Well you should them ken best Lord
You made them like yoursel'

Haud on jist a minute Mo'
It was the First Two that I made
What happened after that Mo'
Is better left unsaid

But let's get back tae business Mo'
I'll smite them wi' disease
Their drugs and penicillin Lord
Wid soon take care o' these

Well I think I'll jist postpone it Mo'
But one day I'll call their bluff
Gie them another Decade Lord
They'll kill each other off.

ON THE BUSES

You can drink a can o' cola
Take a nip or sup a beer
You can sing a bothy ballad, swear an' cuss
You can scoff a curried chicken
An' a' that chinky gear
But how dare you smoke aboard a Cooncil bus

You can scatter pokes an' papers
And empty tins o' juice
Scrawl your name on seats an' cause a fuss
You can have your trannies blairin'
And tear the seats a' loose
But how dare you smoke aboard a Cooncil bus

Tae the Crocks in Cooncil Chambers
Whae sit and make the rules
Aye searching for another way tae fleece
'Ash' and a' their cronies
Will make ye look like fools
So let a body smoke their pipe in peace.

THE HANGOVER

We sup the pints, and down the nips
As if our legs were hollow
Never thinking o' the hangover
That always seems tae follow

The Life an' Soul, the night before
We never heed the warning
And waken up a shrivelled wreck
For work again next morning

With bloodshot eyes, and tender skull
And a heart filled wi' compunction
We stand in dazed disorder
On legs that willnae function

Wi' leathered tongue, we lick our lips
The morning milk we drain
Then mutter that famous well known line
'I'll never dae that again'.

EPITAPHS AND EPIGRAMS

RONALD REAGAN

Under this boulder, with a chip on his shoulder
Lies a Cowboy of wordly repute
The Code of the West, was slung round his waist
And his brains were kept in his boot

THE IRON MAIDEN

Under this tomb, lies the Duchess of Doom
Who for Power and Glory aye lusted
She scorned all around, and when laid in the ground
She defied Auld Nature, and rusted

ARTHUR SCARGILL

In his comfy earthly nest, of bloody-mindedness
Lies a man who often made the quote
Let Democracy aye rule, don't be taken for a fool
But in Union, you're not allowed to vote

IAN McGREGOR

Under this bit land, lies a Yankee hatchet-man
Profit was his only Faith and Creed
The worms will aye feed well
On his large proportioned shell
But they'll never ever penetrate his heid

When Adam told Eve, he was made from the dust
As they strolled through the Garden of Eden
Eve gave the reply, with a glint in her eye
'Then it's a Vacuum Cleaner I'm needin''

When Samson the Strong, asked Delilah what's wrong
It's your strength that's causing me strife
My strength's in my hair, so she scalped gey sair
Then they both led a quiet normal life

The following two verses were sent to a colleague, who had travelled from Coventry on a business trip, when he reached Dundee he was unfortunately hanselled by a seagull.

All the Seagulls in Dundee
When crossing ower the Toon
Are ordered by the S.N.P.
Tae aye fly upside doon

But should they spot a Sassenach
Wandering through their lands
They'll flip their wings, and do their thing
And 'Splat' him where he stands.

THE ISLE OF ARRAN

When others make the 'Annual Race'
Pursuing the sun from place to place
Westwardly, I turn my face
With inward smile
Then speed my way, with utmost haste
To that lovely Isle

An Isle reflecting Nature's moods
Of flowers, ferns, and pine tree woods
All over which the 'Goat Fell' broods
Bare peaked and barren
Where Monks have blessed with Holy Roods
The Isle of Arran

Her history with pride will name
A King, who's struggle seemed in vain
Until he learned to try again
From creature small
Proclaimed his Independent Reign
And Edward's fall

Her Castle Gardens in late Spring
Would make the dullest senses ring
Or cause the hardest heart to sing
Auld Arran's praise
This brilliant scene will always bring
Fond memories

TO A DANDELION

A thousand curses on yer heid
Ye yellow crested stubborn weed
Whae blaws yer parachutin' seed
A' owre the place
How dare ye spread yer blasted breed
And show yer face

The world is full o' parasites
That sponge and leech on us poor mites
They float aroon like stringless kites
Jist like yersel
Whae plant their roots an' claim their rights
And gie us hell

No matter how I reap an' mow
And rax ma back wi' spade an' hoe
Ye lie there waiting doon below
Wi' sniggerin' root
Then like a messenger o' woe
Up ye shoot

It must hae been some drunken Sandy
That christened ye the Lion Dandy
Wi' gnarled leaves an' stems a' bandy
And whiskered heid
I'll keep the Weedo' aye ways handy
And 'SQUIRT'. . . yer deid

THE SOLDIER

What do you fight for, brave soldier
The Colours, the Country, or Pride
I first of all fight for Survival
And then for the Mate at my side

When Death is my constant companion
In some distant and desolate part
When Courage and Honour may falter
The Mate at your side gives you heart

The Medals and Glory come after
Followed by Sorrow and Grief
The Crosses keep growing
The Brass, keep on crowing
While the Heroes, all lie underneath

THE LETTER

Most people know of, or have heard of, the English 'Magna Carta', or the American 'Declaration of Independence', some can even give you the dates when both were signed. It is therefore sometimes very saddening to hear that they have never heard of the Scottish 'Declaration of Arbroath'. What is even more saddening is that some of them are Scots.

Since Man first lifted quill tae ink
And learnt tae read and write
Many words o' wisdom
Have been brought intae the light

Authors penned their literature
Poets, their prose and rhyme
Composers, scribed their lyrics
Historians, the March of Time

But heard ye o' 'The Letter'
Where a Nation took an Oath
A solemn Loyal Promise
'The Declaration o' Arbroath'

The year was Thirteen Twenty
When Robert Bruce was KING
Six years had past since Bannockburn
When he made this Country sing

The Scots drafted up a Letter
And sent it tae Pope John
Declaring Scotland was a Nation
And not and English pawn

'It's not for gold or glory
Or even honour that we've strived
But for Liberty and Freedom
And we will not be denied
For as long as there's a Hundred Scots
Blood pumping in their veins
We'll fight until the last one drops
Than wear the servile chains'

Four years passed before the Scots
Received the Papal Nod
And another four, till Edward Three
Stopped acting like a god

Aye there's many words o' wisdom
In this Wee Nation's growth
But nothing like 'The Letter'
They drafted at Arbroath

STEPS AND STAIRS

Stairs, to a younger person, usually present no problem, but when one reaches middle age, they tend to look like something out of a mountaineering manual, especially the stairs in Edinburgh.

The 'Scotsman Steps' are quite unique
As they wind their draughty trend
The stair is broad, but never steep
But your glad tae reach the end

I've climbed the 'Steps o' Waverley'
The wind whistlin' in my lugs
I've reached the top, without a stop
But 'Blawin' for the Tugs'

The 'Calton' and the 'Castle Stair'
Have likewise bore my tread
And like many a weary pilgrim
I've stood panting at their head

'Fleshmarket Close', I know it well
I'll climb thon stair wi' zest
At 'The Half-Way' up, I'll take my sup
And stagger up the rest

The 'Grassmarket' and the 'Vennel Stairs'
Will rob you o' your puff
On reaching baith their summits
You'll swear enough's, enough

But the 'Stair' that left me gasping
And turned my lungs red raw
That tore the sweat, from out my brow
Are the 'Daddy' o' them a'

They're the 'Steps', up fae Auld Market Street
Alongside Scotland's Bank
When first I stared up at this slope
My heart and stomach sank

But up I went, two at a time
Then slowed it down to one
My heart was nearly burstin'
But my climb was nearly done

At last, wi' tremblin', strawlike legs
I stood, triumphant, at the top
Then turning tae the righthand side
My eyes began tae pop

For there, risin' up in front o' me
Another concrete flight
And I cursed the sadistic planner
Whae had hidden them fae sight

I dragged my shakin' carcass
Step by painful step
Until I reached the Summit
A broken, shattered wreck

As I hung on tae the railings
Blawin' like a train
I took a vow within masel
I'll never climb them again

An auld wife, whae was passin'
Showin' me some concern
Gave these 'Pearls o' Wisdom'
Which everyone should learn

'There's Steps in every City son
And Stairs in every Toon
But the ones here in Auld Reekie
Were made for walkin' DOON'

A MAGICAL NAME

When the zephyr winds of summer
Gently stir the wooded dell
Rustling leaves sigh out in chorus
Ishabel, Ishabel

By the banks of Lomond water
On the shingle and the shell
Ripples break upon the shoreline
Whispering softly Ishabel

Is there a name, that holds such magic
It's rythmn seems to cast a spell
This name belongs in Gaelic folklore
And to a bonnie Balloch Belle

THE MOLE AND THE MOUSE

Never decry anyone less fortunate than yourself, or underestimate the intelligence of a fellow being. If you thirst after success, be nice to people on your way up the ladder, because more than often you'll meet the same people, should you come down.

There was a mouse, that had his nest
Beside a field o' grain
Thinkin' he should hae mair in life
He grew very proud and vain

Why was I, born sae small
He squeaked out at the moon
If I were a lion, or an elephant
I'd sing a different tune

I'd never have tae turn an' flee
From the falcon, hawk, or owl
All I'd need, was tae raise my heid
Flash my teeth, and growl

And a' they stoats, and weasels
That regard me as their lunch
Would scatter, when they saw me
Or underfoot, I'd crunch

And that lightfoot, cunnin', Bushy-Tail
Whae never gies me peace
His days wid a' be numbered
For his hide, and bush, I'd fleece

Now a passing mole, popped up a hole
An' sat listening for a while
Then when the mousie, paused for breath
He spoke up wi' a smile

'Hey cousin, why no' be yersel
Why sit there now and sulk
The best o' gear, we always hear
Aye comes in smaller bulk'

'Now take the lion, and the elephant
They're maybe proud an' tall
But they in turn, are hunted by
The greatest killer of us all'

'This killer, disnae hunt for food
But when he's on the loose
He'll kill an' maim, and kill again
The world's, his slaughter-hoose'

'Aye he's one tae be avoided
For he sometimes turns insane
And just tae satisfy his appetite
He'll turn and kill his ane'

'But you and me, are far too wee
Tae cause Man, any strife
He never seems tae bother
About the little things in life'

'So cousin, stop yer pining
For the things you'll never reach
Be thankful for sma' mercies
An' aye practice what ye preach'

'And remember that the elephant
Whaes built jist like a house
Will shy away in terror
From the sniffin', squeakin', mouse'

The mouse, who had been listening
Shook his head in awe
And wondered how such wisdom
Could come from one sae sma'

He thanked the mole, for his advice
Nae mair wid he moan and grouse
And crawled into his warm wee nest
A humbler, wiser, mouse

THE PYTHAGORAS THEOREM

Could this be the way to make Geometry more interesting?

Auld Pythagoras, had a theorem
That, no one can deny
And the whole world has accepted
That his figures never lie

Take the Square, on the Hypotenuse
And let Scotland's Flag unfurl
It's equal to the sum of Flags
O' any two Countries, o' this World

Now Pythagoras, never realised
The different uses tae his plan
But this Ancient Greek, was quite unique
And he was a clever man

POLLUTIN' MAN

Man will colonize the Moon, and in doing so, will pollute it

Man has walked on Lunar Dust
In his germ free space cocoon
But come the day, when breathe or burst
Man will pollute the moon

COMPLICATED MAN

Some men don't know what they want, or what side to take, therefore one never knows whether to trust or mistrust them. They lead a Jekyll and Hyde existence.

Of all the life upon this Earth
There's nothing stranger than
The sometimes saintly, sometimes devious
Complicated Man

CHARITABLE MAN

To practice charity, when one can afford it financially, is a worthy gesture, but to practice charity when one can't afford it, is a sign of true greatness.

A man that has Faith, will reign as a Prince
Midst the 'Flot and Jet' of humanity
But a man is a King of all he surveys
If that man practices Charity

POLITICAL MAN

POLITICIANS, no matter what their beliefs, are a breed of people on their own, and there are very few I would trust, but this is only my opinion

An honest man, the Bard has said
Is the noblest work of God
Tho' his life be one long struggle
He walks where Saints have trod

But where walks the Politician
We only can surmise
One thing for sure, he'll never walk
The Paths of Paradise

Left, or Right, or half-way roun'
No matter what his creed
They'll preach and plan, at our expense
Tae satisfy their greed

THE PUB PHILOSOPHER

Since we joined the Common Market, it seemed that every time I read a newspaper, someone from the European Community would be informing us that the Scots were either smoking too much, or eating and drinking too much. Scotland and the Scots became the Aunt Sally for every journalist and politician striving to find fame in his or her own particular field. This poem, is a discussion in a pub between two mates or cronies, who give their own criticism, reasoning, and final analysis, which is, 'Wha daur meddle wi' us'.

Have another dram Jock
For it maybe be our last
The Common Market experts
Have been digging in our past

They claim we're a' addicted
Tae the whisky, wine and beer
But whae are they tae tell us
The wife's been saying that for years

Have they ever sat like us Jock
Savouring the tang
Sharing each other's troubles
Or danced and roared and sang

Aye, we'll hae another dram Jock
An' tae hell wi' what they've said
If we a' gie up the drinking
They'll be taxing milk instead

Have another fag Jock
It's a low tae middle tar
And again the so-called experts
Once mair put up the bar

It seems the Scots a' smoke too much
We're addicted tae the snout
But tae tell the honest truth Jock
I cannae stub them out

Man, how could we miss each morning
When we take the day's first draw
Then cough, tae we near turn purple
And gasp out 'That wis braw'

Aye, if we a' gie up the smoking
And they close the baccy shops
I'm certain where they'll shift the tax
The sweets and lollipops

Forget the 'Sunday Dinner' Jock
We're putting on the weight
If we don't cut down the calories
It's gaun tae be too late

Nae mair tripe or stovies
Nae haggis, fish and chips
Nae mair mince an' tatties
Nae mair walnut whips

Man, they're gaun their dinger
Trying tae impress
An' jist like Shetland Ponies
They'll hae us eating gress

Our teeth are a' gaun bad they say
The Scots are a' gaun gummy
There's only one thing for it Jock
Forget the honey, dummy

One thing is for sure Jock
The whole o' life's a cancer
And a' they so-called experts
Still have nae found an answer

We bawl for breath, the day we're born
And gasp for it when we're dyin'
And the only thing that's in between
Is the laughin' and the cryin'

But when this country, needs you
And a' systems are at go
The boozin', cancerous, gummy Scot
Is aye the FIRST tae go

THE GRASS ROOTS

Most people think St. Andrews
Is the stately home o' Gowf
And the title 'Royal Ancient', they bequeath
But the 'Place' where it all started
In a wee-bit wooden Howff
Was on the Public Links o' Sunny Leith

THE TRAMP

We tend to look down with disdain, or to avoid any contact with a tramp, but underneath those rags might beat a warm and friendly heart.

I met a man the other day
No ordinary man I might well say
Whae viewed the world in his own sweet way
And tae me seemed quite contented

I first saw him on a public seat
And at his side, a bundle neat
Open sandals on his feet
And his claes had been 'presented'

I took a seat and said hello
And watched his eyes begin tae glow
The conversation began tae flow
Our friendship seemed cemented

'Some call me hobo, travelling man
Some tramp, or Gaberlunzie man
Others a roadway gentleman
These names I've not resented'

'Some gie me work, an' pay me well
Some pass the time, jist like yersel'
Some want me locked up in a cell
Sometimes I'm fair demented'

'Four walls I've never found appealing
The cities hustle leaves me reeling
The stars have always been my ceiling
Maist times I'm fair contented'

'Auld Nature can be friend or foe
She plans the times tae reap or sow
She'll bless wi' sun, or curse wi' snow
She's one tae be respected'

'I've tramped Auld Scotland wi' a smile
Embracing every scenic mile
I've always thought it well worthwhile
And never felt neglected'

'So whatever happens, come what may
Through summer blue, or winter grey
I draw warmth and comfort every day
With the memories I've collected'

We parted then, said our goodbyes
The glowing warmth still in his eyes
And for years to come, I'll always prize
The memories he reflected

SIMPLE PLEASURES

Everyone has something, be it a certain sound, or odour, that reminds them of a time in their past which gave them a moments pleasure. It is usually the simplest things that give the most pleasure. Could it be one of these?

When one is asked, for the smallest things
That give the greatest pleasure
The simplest things aye spring tae mind
Things we always treasure

The smell o' fresh cut pinewood
Brings back by-gone days
O' camp fires, tents, and saw-mills
And boyhood memories

Church bells ringing on a Sunday morn
A sound that's sure tae please
And the smell o' streaky bacon
Wafting on the breeze

A new laid tarmacadam road
Freshly raked and rolled
The smell o' the tarry boiler
Is worth it's weight in gold

The sight of an old-time sailing ship
It's canvas, puffed out by the wind
Ploughing it's way, through foamy seas
It's a pleasure, that springs tae mind

Then, of course, another sight
I'm sure will never fade
The massed Pipe Bands of Scotland
Marching on parade

But the simplest of all pleasures
Yet the greatest one I'd say
Is to waken up each morning
And start another day

INEQUALITY

The word is self explanatory, this country has it the world is full of it, and it doesn't look as if it ever will change.

Why worry about dying
When living's hard enough
Why dream o' the hereafter
When the present claims your worth

Preachers, priests and clergy
Content tae play their role
Will disregard the body
But try an' save the soul

Their churches stand half empty
It appears they don't know why
They preached, Hellfire an' brimstone
And the price was much too high

Money now is worshipped
Among the titled ranks
Their Cathedral is the Stock-Exchange
Their Churches now, the Banks

The rich man buys his titles
The poor man buys his bread
An' never the twain shall meet in life
They're only equal when they're dead

Small wonder why the poorer class
Shake their heads in wonder
They're promised Kingdoms when they die
Up there in the wild blue yonder

But a Christian still can worship God
Without visiting a church
A heathen practice charity
Sometimes giving twice as much

When bread was but the staff o' life
We dreamed o' milk and honey
The dream is gone and in its place
It's money, money, money

Police and politicians tell us
Crime will never pay
But M.P.'s, cops and robbers
Prove it does, near' every day

But come the day, and it will I pray
When like Sodom and Gomorrah
The Lord will call enough's enough
And we'll have a new tomorrow

Aye ashes tae ashes, dust tae dust
The last words sound distressing
But when it comes, as come it must
Tae some it will be a blessing

THE ELMS O' REEKIE

Dutch Elm disease hit Edinburgh like a blight and it seems like the only cure is to chop them down then burn them. While they are doing this lets hope they have the foresight to plant other trees in their place, there's an old saying, 'You never miss the water till the well runs dry'.

Scolytus damned Scolytus
That deadly foreign bug
A thousand curses on yer heid
For biting 'Reekie's' lug

Running rampant doon in England
Ye gorged for a' your worth
Then filtered in unnoticed
Tae the 'Athens o' the North'

Ye chewed your way through Princes Street
An unseen, creeping, cancer
And a' the brains in Britain
Still havenae found an answer

Oh the bonnie Elms o' Reekie
Have been riddled like a cheese
And now are slowly dying off
Fae that 'Dutchy Elm' disease

What would 'Auld Reekie' look like
Without Elms in her Main Street
They blend wi' a' her statues
And make the view complete

So start planting wi' the Sycamore
The Planetree, Beech and Lime
For the bonnie Elms o' Reekie
Are running short o' time

NATIONAL SERVICE

The points for or against 'National Service' will always be argued, but what it did do, was give an education in the University of Life to every young man who was ever 'Called Up' into it.

It was blanco and blacken
Brasso and bull
Yes sir, and no sir
An' three kit-bags full

Your constant companions
A knife fork and spoon
An' a big slab o' concrete
Where ye marched up and doon

A bull-neckit sergeant
Wi' a voice like a horn
Whae aye made ye wish
Ye had never been born

Trained wi' a rifle
Tae shoot enemies deid
By the time ye were finished
Ye'd a' shot him insteid

Yer boots spit an' polished
Till the wrinkles had gone
Yer heid shaved like a tumshie
Right doon tae the bone

Put through yer paces
Time after time
The 'FIRST O' THE FOOT'
And 'RIGHT O' THE LINE'

The 'Bouncers o' Pilate'
The pride o' the lan'
Ye went in a boy
An' came oot a man

STEMS

Stems is an abbreviation for Scottish Technical Education Modules which is a new fangled jargon used to-day, to teach 1st and 2nd year pupils in school, Woodwork, Metalwork and Technical Drawing. This new jargon together with the banning of the 'Lochgelly Tawse', has in my opinion only lead to both the teacher and the pupil becoming more confused, and set education as we used to know it, down a steep and slippery slope. However I've used the word Stems in another form and compared it to the world of Horticulture, i.e. plants etc.

The Stems o' any plant or shrub
Will produce some bonny shoots
But the strength o' any healthy growth
Aye lies within the roots

But the roots o' Education
Have dried up like the straw
And the Flowers o' this Wee Nation
Are a' weed awa

The blossoms a' were tested
In last years Flower Show
And the results o' a the Prelims
Are given down below

A Cramp, is very painful
A Bit, is very brief
A Bowsaw, fires arrows
And a Brace goes round your teeth

A Tenon, is a muscle
You might think this all absurd
But what do you think a Dovetail is?
Yes, the back end of a bird

Copper, is a polisman
Sheet Metal, they call tin
Zinc, you fill with water
And wash your dishes in

Mention Pyramids, and Prisms
And they turn away or hide
But given a brand new Drawing Board
They'll carve their name with pride

The root of all their problems
Is known to all I'm sure
That when planting the Seed of Knowledge
You must use the right manure

One must fertilize with Discipline
And rake out a' the weeds
Pruning back, the Maverick Growth
Tae encourage Healthy Seeds

And when talking to the Flowering Plants
As many people do
Use simple, common, language
And they'll always trust in you.

THE GOLDEN ANSWER

If all the powerful countries
Signed a Treaty made to hold
That a' their nuclear weapons
Would be made from solid gold

There wouldnae be sae many bombs
Tae hand out tae their mates
And a' those itchy fingers
Wid be scratching worried pates

There would never be a stockpile
Nae fear o' nuclear strike
With the smaller nations calling out
Bomb us if you like

For if by chance they let one go
No matter where it fell
Midst a' the devastation
There'd be gold dust there as well

THE PENICUIK PUSHER

A good friend of mine, Bob Solway, is sometimes bothered with his stomach. He carries a small container of Sodium Bicarbonate which now and again, he takes a small dose. It seems to work wonderfully well, and he'll gladly give anyone suffering from heartburn etc., a small drop of this miracle cure, Bob lives in Penicuik, hence the title.

There is a man among us
Bob Solway is his name
They call him the Penicuik Pusher
And he's grown gey rich in fame

If you hae a touch o' heartburn
Or your stomach's turning sour
Take my tip, and see our Bob
And your troubles will be owre

His hand dips in his pooches
His eyes dart, side tae side
Then oot he draws, the magic box
And his face lights up wi' pride

He taps the box twice on the lid
Chanting oot a spell
They say he learnt it fae a witch
Whae stayed in Colinton Dell

'Haud oot your hand, he'll order ye
And for God's sake, dinnae cough
He'll drop some powder on your palm
Then tell ye, 'Lick it off''

You'll feel your stomach rumbling
And your shaking at the knee
Then out it comes a mighty belch
And you mumble 'Pardon me'

I asked Bob, 'What's the secret
That cures the painful kyte'
'There isnae any secret man
It's powdered dynamite'

'I never touch the stuff masel
It always makes me choke'
'What dae you hae then ?' says I
'I'll hae a rum an' coke'

'Dae they never hae an accident
When they use that powerful stuff'
'Aye, one bloke belched too hard one time
And blew his eyebrows off'

So if your paunch is poorly
Or you play it just for kicks
Go find the Penicuik Pusher
And ask him for a 'fix'

KIRSTY'S CHRISTENING TOAST

Dedicated to our first grandchild Kirsty, and which I recited at her christening in the form of a toast.

There's many a wonder in this world
That Nature's hand has styled
But there's none that give more pleasure
Than the cry of a new-born child

When held in the sweet contentment
Of a mother's fond embrace
We behold a loving portrait
Of tenderness and grace

A boy, a girl, it matters not
Each have their personal claim
But today, the toast is Kirsty
A guid auld Scottish name

May fortune always smile on her
And happiness be her guide
May she live a life, aye free o' strife
And carry her name with pride

To all who gathered here today
At the christening o' this babe
Let's lift our glass, and drink a toast
To bonnie wee Kirsty McCabe

ADDRESS TO MY GRANDSON 'LAWRIE'

Dedicated to our grandson Lawrie, the first laddie in our family.

Under the sign of Capricorn
One January night
A strappin' laddie once was born
A warm and welcome sight

He had his faither's features braw
And his mother's bronze lit hair
He'll be a credit tae us a'
Could we ask for any mair

Some Lords and Dukes hae titles grand
Which can be bought or sold
But 'Lawrie Manclark Crosbie', man
That's a title tae behold

And when asked about your title lad
And why the meaning o' it
Tell them, Crosbie was your faither's name
And Manclark was a poet

Ye'll hae your share o' happiness son
And ye'll hae your share o' strife
But aye make honesty and sincerity
The true anchors o' your life

THE MOANER

Moaner McGubb, aye complained in the club
That the beer was always too weak
Don't mess about, get Strongbow, he'd shout
Until the barman got seak

So they sent down an order, tae South o' the Border
For a keg o' this guid cider brew
And when Moaner came in, he started tae grin
When he saw the 'Strongbow' on view

At last ye've shown sense, tae hell wi' the expense
Gies a pint o' that guid applejack
But as he lifted his glass, it then came tae pass
Two ARROWS thudded in tae his back

EDINBURGH

When one looks down, on Edinburgh Town
From the heights o' Arthur Seat
And a thousand years o' History
Lie there at your feet
A humble man, can only stand
And marvel at the scene
For there lies the Queen of the Lowlands
The Flower of the Scottish Dream

On summer days in sunny June
When flowers and shrubs are in full bloom
And the air is heavy with perfume
In fair Dunedin
Beneath the City's bustling tune
There lies an Eden

A garden sprung, from Auld Nor' Loch
Sheltered by the Castle Rock
That boasts a plant-filled Floral Clock
And lush green grass, Where silent statues, all take stock
On all who pass

MOTHERHOOD

Of all the Wonders in this World
Which Nature's Hand has styled
There's none that give more pleasure
Than the cry of a new born child

When held in the sweet contentment
Of a mother's fond embrace
A peaceful, loving, portrait
Of tenderness and grace

Her eyes, hold that inquiring glance
And clear as crystalled waters
Her smile, makes all her dimples dance
The Mother of my daughters

SOMEONE'S MISSING

George Shoemark, an ex-miner, and a poetical friend of mine, wrote this poem 'Someone's Missing', it is a great wee poem in my opinion, but I felt that maybe using local dialect, the scene could be described more dramatically without altering the structure of the poem. George requested that I do this and it is with his kind permission, that the poem appears below. The poem is entirely his, I was only glad to help.

I was drenched and drowning
In my own sweat, lying
In my stint of unstripped coal
And old moleskin clothes
In a wet shallow seam.
Then, as in a dream,
I saw orange clad shapes coming
Towards me, their dipping, bobbing
Lamps in single file, shuffling,
Coughing, dying on the· feet.
Anxiously, I counted. . .
Tam
Airchie
Sandy
Someone's late—
Jock
Willie
Rab
Shuggie
Aleck—
Someone's missing—
That's only eight.

There I was
Lying in mou'wart breeks and sark
Droukit, drownin' in my ain sweat
Howkin' coal, in a wet shallow seam
Daen my stint
In Auld Nick's Kingdom.

Then, as in a dream
I made out shapes
Coming towards me, in single file
Lamps dippin' and bobbin'
Feet shufflin', coughin'
Pechin' and pantin'
Raxin' their lungs for air
On they came, near dyin' on their feet
Anxiously I counted. . .
Tam—Airchie—Sandy—
Whaes that? aye it's Wullie—
Rab—Shuggie—Alec—Jock—
Someone's missin'—
That's only eight. . .

Droukit—Drenched
Mou'wart—Moleskin
Sark—Shirt
Howkin'—Digging
Raxin'—Stretching
Pechin'—Wheezing

A REMEDY

There is no harm in trying this, who knows, it may help.

When everything is going wrong
When days seem short, and nights are long
You have a feeling you don't belong
Then use your imagination

Let your brain slip into gear
Drain your heart, until it's clear
Purge your mind o' doubt and fear
With determined concentration

Then as the thoughts drift by your eyes
Select the ones you'll always prize
Reject the ones you now despise
Without any hesitation

Now let each thought, each new found treasure
Return within, at your own leisure
Savour the ones that give most pleasure
With careful calculation

If this has changed the black to grey
Shortened the night, and lengthened the day
There's only one thing more to say
Laugh in celebration

THE KIDNAPPING O' PETER THE METER

This poem is dedicated to the President and Members of the Baillieston Bowling Club who on their annual visit to our Club, presented to me, a full size Parking Meter with a concrete base, and the words 'Peter the Meter', printed on it. 'Peter' now stands in the Edinburgh Bowling Club.

I was standing in the Canongate
One quiet and moonlight night
When a big, black, shiny Limousine
Suddenly cruised in sight
It parked itsel' right next tae me
It must have weighed a ton
Then oot jumped two masked muggers
Armed wi' a Kango Gun

They blasted up the pavement
Then cut doon through my root
And covered wi' a plastic bag
They bunged me in the boot
Then off we sped tae Glesgae
Turning right at Baillieston Cross
And in a dingy room, in the Bowling Club
They introduced me to the Boss

He was known as 'Presidento'
He had teeth like half-inch tacks
His face was full o' badges
And his eyes like Bowling Jacks
He spoke in a funny dialect
That was hard tae understand
He must have come fae Paisley
Or maybe Anniesland

His henchmen grabbed a haud o' me
Their eyes like blackened slits
One o' them looked like Brando
The other like Zasu Pitts
They filled me up wi' foreign coins
Tae guddle up my brain
I'd never been fed like that before
I felt like a party wean

Then in came two auld Boolers
Whae must have played as skips
For they battered me wi' 'Hensilites'
But I never moved my lips
'Haud on', yelled Presidento
As he chewed a piece o' chalk
'They've taen us a' for suckers
This meter cannae talk'

So they buried my feet in concrete
And I can assure you pal
I then thought I was headin'
For the Forth and Clyde Canal
But the Bossman then decided
As he gave his chins a rub
'Take it back tae that Bammy Poet
In the Edinburgh Bowling Club'

So they brought me back fae Glesgae
When they came tae play 'The Game'
And man, I can only tell ye
It was great tae be hame again

I now stand in the Edinburgh Club
In a corner o' my ain
And I listen tae the banter
As the Boolers play their game
It's warmer than the Canongate
Nae winds aroond yer lugs
A guid auld friendly atmosphere
And best of all, NAE DUGS

You'll never hear me talk much
The reason is quite plain
If that Glesgae mob get wind o' it
They'll hi-jack me again.

A GUID SCOT'S FRIEND

There's many a Scot
And I've met quite a lot
Whose friendship I still carry
But the 'Truest Blue'
That I ever knew
Was a plumber called Jock Barrie

Like a' guid Scots
He has his fauts
But a heart o' carat gold
Fate changed her plan
When she made this man
Then threw away the mould

As Secretary of the Edinburgh Bowling Club, I found that, following complaints, if I wrote the Notices in rhyme and pinned them on the Notice Board, more Members read them and the message was also put across.

KEEP THE HEID

When all around are losing theirs
Aye try and keep the heid
It's nice tae be nice
You never live twice
And man,. . . your a long time deid

VISITORS

When signing in a visitor
Aye take a second look
Make sure their money's in the box
And their names are in the book

COMPLAINTS

The Edinburgh Club is a friendly wee club
And we aye try tae keep it that way
If you have a complaint
Be you sinner or saint
Put it in writing today

BE UP

Lachie McFort, always bowled short
And his skip always cried 'Dearie Me'
'Am I up ?' he would cry
And his skip would reply
'They're nearer tae you than tae me'

KEEP OFF

We know Bowling is a tiring game
And you love to rest your shanks
But keep your feet of a' rink edges
And your 'Bums' of a' the banks

THE PLYMOUTH CANNONBOWL

Sir Francis Drake, was aye wide awake
When playing in a Bowling Cup
When The Armada it came
He finished his game
But only because he was up

He lost tie, but never say die
Francis was never beat
He fired his bowls through the cannons
And sank the whole Spanish Fleet

The Spaniards learnt weel
They have now bowls of steel
Which they throw at a small metal 'Jack'
And stamped on it's face, is Drake's bearded face
In this way they get their ain back

THE AIMS OF MEMBERS

Following complaints from the Vice President, about the floor of the Gents toilet always being wet, the following poem was put up on the wall, and to some extent, proved successful.

This 'Trough' was placed by worthy craftsmen
And is firmly anchored doon
How the hell you seem tae miss it
Always baffles Jimmy Broon

Some bowlers can, wi' great precision
'Touch a Jack' while bowling neat
But shakin' hands wi' 'Auld John Thomas'
'Trough' and 'Thomas', never meet

Those of you, whilst in 'The Forces'
Army, Navy, or Flying School
Followed the drill of Target Practice
Always obeyed the Golden Rule

Point the Weapon at the Target
Take your aim wi' beady eye
Fire the Weapon, hit Dead Centre
Close the Breech, and then stand by

When standing here wi' good intentions
And your mission's near complete
Don't look up towards the ceiling
You could be 'Pissing' on your feet

THE BOWLING GAME

Though I'm not what you may call an expert bowler, I'm never the less a keen one, and I always look forward eagerly to the Bowling Season which begins in April every year. I can honestly think of no other game where the atmosphere, although competitive, is so friendly. It doesn't matter whether you are old or young, you can still take part, and it is one of the less expensive sports still open to people, especially O.A.P.s.

Now some men claim that fishing
Is the greatest sport of all
Others choose tae trudge a course
Skelpin' a wee white ball

But may I say with no offence
Each man tae his tools
But gie tae me, a summer's day
And a friendly game o' 'Bools'

When 'Boolin' Fever' catches you
Your world begins tae change
You speak a different language
And your actions tae are strange

The rules are all quite simple
And easily understood
The 'Jack' is called the 'Sweetie'
And the 'Bool' is called the 'Wood'

All the Bools are biased
The means they're weighted tae one side
And if they're no' held properly
They'll dae a 'Palais Glide'

The 'Skip' instructs the Boolers
Wi' signs and shouts galore
Like a 'polis' guiding traffic
Or a sailor's Semaphore

'Mair grass', he'll shout out tae ye
Or 'You're coming in too high'
Then quickly dodges out the road
As the Bools go whizzing by

One 'Skip' I know, turned up one day
Wi' cricket pads an' all
I asked him why the kinky gear
He said 'We're playing Danderhall'

'How's my Bools' I asked a Skip
Trying hard tae please
'If I was you I'd burn them son
They've got Dutch Elm Disease'

But when your Skip is smiling
And no' chewing at his hat
You'll know your Bools are running well
And you proudly leave the mat

Four 'ends' up, they open the Bar
And the Boolers slake their thirst
Trottin' off in pairs they go
Startin' wi' the First

Then in and out, each in their turn
Until it comes tae pass
They get mair 'Loaded' than their 'Bools'
And therefore use mair grass

When the 'Game' is over
And your Skip says you've done weel
Baith Teams trudge intae the Club
And sit down tae a meal

In this warm and friendly atmosphere
Baith sides gie three cheers
There's nae losers in this company
Amidst the nips an' beers

When the Season's ended
And you pack away your 'Gear'
You'll try an' find a substitute
Till it starts again next year

But fae nineteen up tae ninety
No' matter what your age
You'll never find a substitute
Boolin's aye the 'Rage'

STRONG DRINK

A measure nip, taen sip by sip
Will stimulate the brain
Taen by the glass
You'll use mair grass
And probably lose the game

SPILLER MILLER

In a Bowling Club in Meadow Lane
There sits a man there on his ain
Whae plays a different kind o' game
They call him 'Spiller Miller'

Now many men are gifted
And their deeds might make ye blink
But few are ever famous
In the art o' Spilling Drink

Such a man was 'Spiller'
Who's fame spread far and near
The very mention o' his name
Had grown men white wi' fear

He'd sit among the Members
And they could lay a bet
That before he ever rose again
They'd a' be soaken wet

Lager, Heavy, Black an' Tan
Or any beer on tap
One unguarded moment
And your pint was on your lap

A flicking wrist, an elbow nudge
This crafty game he'd play
With deadly calm precision
He could even 'Heid' a tray

Aye Spiller was a craftsman
On that you aye could tell
For in all his spilling escapades
Nane landed on himsel'

His wife an' bairns a' tell me
And I'm sure they speak the truth
That when sittin' down at mealtimes
They a' wear waterproofs

But the Members found an answer
Tae curb his deadly skills
For every pint that Spiller spilt
They ordered 'Quarter Gills'

Spiller has been 'cured' now
And the members calm their nerves
But when they see him in the Club
They still dae 'body swerves'

ODE TO BILLY BROWN

This is a poem sent to a friend, Billy Brown, who is a joiner to trade, and who promised to replace my front door.

There's a door doon in Glenvarloch
That is creakin' wi' auld age
Baith it's hinges and it's locks are slackened sair
It keeps groanin' for retirement
And rattlin' wi' rage
It's panels are a' cracked, wi' wear an' tear

Now there's a busy little joiner
Whae hails fae Bellenden
He's an expert on retiring creakin' doors
He promised a replacement
The only question's when
So my wife an' I are praying on all fours

THE PRAYER

O ye whae rules the Heavens
The Forests and the Trees
And a' the Doors an' Windaes in The Inch
A small request we're askin'
Doon on bended knees
And wi' a' Your Power an' Glory, it's a cinch

Clutch the breeks o' that wee joiner
Check the Wind, and use Your Might
An' punt him skywards, near tae where we're livin'
If your Judgement's Worthy
He should land direct on site
At the gates o' Glenvarlochy Ninety-Seven

If the prayer fails, then drastic measures must be taken.

THE CURSE O' THE BARD O' GLENVARLOCH

May yer Chisels turn tae rubber
And yer Hammers turn tae glass
Yer Saw-Blades lose their teeth, an' rust away
May yer Planes become a' maukit
Then may it come tae pass
That the Putty in yer windaes, turn tae clay

May yer Nails a' bend and buckle
And yer Screws reverse their thread
Yer Varnish tins a' burst across yer floor
May ye stand amang the chaos
And wished never said
That ye'd come and change The Manclark's Auld Front Door.

PROUDLY SING

There are too many people nowadays who spend most of their time running Scotland down. Ever since the Romans tried to conquer this Country, and up to the present day, we are ruled by division. We have been brainwashed for hundreds of years, all supposedly for our own good, and slowly, but surely, we are losing our history, culture, literature, and language, and most of all, our pride.

O sing the songs of Scotland's Story
Sing them in your Native Tongue
Tap your feet tae 'Tunes o' Glory'
Skirled out by the Pipes and Drums

Shed the tears of pure emotion
Unashamed, let loose the flood
A Nation built on sheer devotion
Her History made with Flesh and Blood

Sing of Sons in lonely places
Sing o' families ower the sea
Scotia how my heart embraces
Land of Heroes, hame tae me

Caledonia's Congregation
Loudly sing your Country's fame
Raise your voices in vibration
Proudly speak, Auld Scotland's name

THE GLENVARLOCH BEACON

There's a door down in Glenvarloch
That the neighbours cannot pass
A structure of perfection
Of mahogany and brass

It shines out like a beacon
And I'm sure it always will
Thanks to a friendly joiner
And his artistry and skill

THE LUCKY SEVEN BINGO CLUB

In Rabbie's days, they had nae clubs
And drank in dingy Inns or Pubs
They whiled away their idle time
Suppin' beer, and Claret wine

And a' their guid wives stayed at hame
Working their fingers tae the bane
Scrubbing flairs and tendin' weans
And getting nothing for their pains

But times have changed, and so have wives
The Numbers Game, now rules their lives
History has turned a page
And 'Bingo' now, is a' the rage

On Friday nights, at the 'Lucky Seven'
When a' the cards are paid and given
They sit in rows and drink their gin
And wait the call, 'Eyes Down' - 'Look In'

The game begins, the balls a' rattle
They sit there a' prepared for battle
Pencils poised, eyes on their card
And the chant begins, fae the Bingo Bard

All the Fours, it's Forty-Four
Two and One, that's Key o' the Door
On it's own, it's Lucky Seven
All the Ones, That's Legs Eleven

Ower their cards, they sit and browse
Then up jumps one, and shouts out 'House'
And a wifie nearby, bangs her broo
'Ahm only waitin' on number two'
Another smirks, and points her pencil
'She's had mair hooses, than the Local Cooncil'

And on it goes, a' through the night
Man, it's such an unco sight
They stay there tae the final bell
And they seem tae a' enjoy thersel'

Such pleasures are sae few tae find
And life is just a daily grind
So if Bingo cheers, then what the Hell
Get out and play, and enjoy yersel'

AULD REEKIE'S VOICE

The One O'clock Gun fires every day from Edinburgh Castle at 1p.m. to inform people in Edinburgh and the surrounding districts, that it is indeed One O'clock (1300hrs.)

On the Ramparts o' The Castle
High above the moat
At a certain time on every day
Auld Reekie clears her throat

At the Thirteenth Hour, or more precise
When the Tron Kirk Clock strikes one
A rolling 'Boom', a puff o' smoke
The Voice o' the One O'clock Gun

The Time Ball on the Calton Hill
It's upward climb being done
Plummets downward in salute
Tae the Voice o' the One O'clock Gun

Every Starling, Spag, and Pidgeon
Rise tae the skies as one
Then fly in close formation
By command o' the One O'clock Gun

So here's a Toast tae The Voice o' Reekie
May it never be struck dumb
May it aye ring oot, in braw salute
The Voice o' the One O'clock Gun

A LETTER FAE AULD REEKIE

The Edinburgh Street Fronts, have changed dramatically over the past few years, and sad to say the change has been for the worse. Some of the shops that once thrived, are now lying derelict or boarded up. The following lines can be sung to the tune of 'The Mountains of Mourn', strangely enough.

Dear Johnnie Auld Reekie
Has lost her respect
Wi' shops lying empty
An' dying o' neglect

The Street o' The Princes
Is lookin' two-faced
On one side there's beauty
On the other disgrace

The North and South Bridges
Are covered in shame
And everyone tells me
The Rates are tae blame

There's Pizzas and Popshops
Boutiques and Bazaars
Bookies and Bingo
And dingy wee Bars

The people are changing
They've lost all their glow
Their Pride and their Passion
Are burning quite low

The young ones in warpaint
And hair standing strecht
Some shaved like a tumshie
Fae foreheid tae neck

The Jewel o' the Lowlands
Has lost a' her shine
And we just sit in sorrow
Remembering Lang Syne

So for a' that you'll see here
You might as well be
On the Bass Rock at Berwick
Or the Slopes o' Glenshee

AULD REEKIE RIGHT OR WRANG

There has always been a friendly rivalry between the two cities of Edinburgh and Glasgow, on which is the better city. The following rhymes were written with tongue in cheek, to a very good friend of mine, John Black of Bishopriggs, who incidentally blends his own whisky for personal use, which is typical of a Glaswegian. This is an answer to his first friendly jibe.

In the Capital o' Scotland John
Where history was made
Auld Reekie shines in glory John
And puts Glesga in the shade

Even the Guid Book tells us John
A fact that stands the test
That the Wise Men aye came fae the East
And the Fly-Men fae the West

But haud yer wheesht guid Johnnie lad
And listen tae what I say
You'll maybe learn a thing or two
Upon this very day

When Glesga wis a spec o' dust
An' the Clyde, a wee bit stream
Auld Reekie bloomed on Scotia's Crust
The Flower o' the Scottish Dream

And the Learned Men o' this Fair Toon
A' gathered tae decide
Tae spread their knowledge and their skill
Across the Country wide

They built a road tae Glesga John
And sent Saint Mungo owre fae Fife
Tae educate Glaswegians
On the neccessities o' life

Glesga's flourished since John
An' grown tae quite a size
But in comparison wi' us John
Ye take the Second Prize

Aye each tae his ain city John
The feelings aye run strang
But I'll stand wi' burstin' heart an' shout
Auld Reekie, right or wrang

GLESGA'S MILES BETTER

This was the reply from John Black, using the 'Glasgow's Miles Better' slogan, which was introduced by Provost Michael Kelly to publicise Glasgow as a tourist attraction, and which was seemingly very successful.

Am scunnered fair the day, tae get
Yir Edinburgh Epistle
Fu o' Reekie blethers an' conceit
Enough tae mak me whustle

There's nae doot in ma mind Dave
Yir daen yir best tae try us
Sae staun aboon the Waverely Steps
An' blaw away yir bias

The fresh air howling every hour
Should clear awa the drooth
That's cloggin' up yir thinking power
O' facts that are the truth

Ye rant an' rave Auld Reekie's praise
Fae Arthur's Seat ye smile
Wi' Castle high fur Tourist gaze
An' Palace doon the Mile

Yir Prince's Street it used tae be
A place fur folks tae staun
But there's muckle else tae see
It's pride and prestige gaun

O' a' the toons ye care tae name
Frae Timbuctoo tae Brest
Ye must admit wi' unco shame
Auld Glesga's still the best

Wi' a' yir fancy talk this while
Yir heid's gaun roon an' roon
The only thing ye've got worthwhile
Is the road tae Glesga Toon

Sae next ye meet a Glesga frien'
Low born or man o' letters
Lift yir hat an' bow yir heid
In the company o' yir betters

The plight o' Auld Reekie
Wid make a body froon
But the pride o' them a', Is still Glesga Toon.

EDINA'S MUCH FINER

The reply to John Black's 'Glesga's Miles Better', Edina is another name for Edinburgh.

The plight o' guid Auld Reekie John
As ye say, is sair tae bear
An' wi' the Festival and Fringes
It's like the Glesga Fair

They're dancing in the streets here John
An' naebody's complainin'
but the 'Winos' in St. Enoch Square
Are far mair entertaining

But nae matter what the trauchel John
We must earn our daily breid
No' like yer Glesga Council
Whae must be aff their heid

Tak' yer keely Mayor Kelly John
And his Band o' Merry Men
Buildin' flats for 'Chopper' Barratt
In the Park o' Rouken Glen

Aye Glesga's miles better John
Or so the slogans say
But the punters arnae laughing
Doon Rouken Park I'd say

Aye we've tourists by the thousands John
Fae Joppa tae Japan
An' they always keep repeatin'
Auld Reekie's 'Number Wan'

If chance I meet a Glesga frien'
I'll take him by the haun
And show him roon the Capital
For he'll no' ken where tae gaun

Aye for me the fecht is sair John
But it's no' the same for you
You can always daunder hame
And sup yer home-made brew

Then lost in that Scotsman's dream world
Ye can toast wi' a touch o' class
Twa fingers tae the Cooncil
An' three fingers tae each glass

Of a' the cities in this world
Fae Canada tae China
Glesga's Miles Better John
But Edina's That Much Finer

REPLY TO NICKY FISHER

A very young teenager, whom I have never met, and who, after reading my poetry, sent me the following two letters in rhyme. It must have taken great deliberation and courage on her part to do this, therefore I posted off replies in rhyme, but as you can see, I made the mistake of thinking Nicky was a LADDIE, and was reprimanded for it.

Dear Mr D Manclark
I've sent ye this wee rhyme
It's not exactly perfect
'Cause I didnae hae much time

My uncle Jim came round last week
And gied me this wee book
I like to write a rhyme mysel'
So I had a butcher's hook

'Twas by a bloke ca'd Manclark
I said 'Christ whae is he?'
(Well you're not yet as famous
As Rabbie Burns ye see!)

But I read the book through anyway
From eight to one hundred and three
And they were more of an inspiration
Than Rabbie ever was tae me

When I read them for the 2nd time
I knew ye were no clown
And your love was as strong as mine
For Auld Reekie, oor home town

The only thing that saddened me
About your book Manclark
Was when ma' Uncle Jim came roond
Asking for it back!

Another thing that bothers me is
Can't the Cooncil builders catch you
I want to ken exactly when
They're starting on your statue

I hope that I've conveyed my thanks
In this short and simple line
And I hope you'll go on writing poems
Until the end of time

Yours sincerely
NICKY FISHER (age 16)

(P.S. If you see my Uncle Jim
Please don't tell him that I wrote
For I like to keep myself you see
As a very private poet!)

97 Glenvarloch Crescent
Edinburgh EH16 6BB

12th May 1986

A thousand blessings on yer heid
Young stalwart o' the rhyming breed
Whilst reading ower yer welcome letter
Ye made my day that wee bit better

The News is full o' Earls and Dukes
And pimps an' drugs, an' thieves an' crooks
Some politicians in the soup
And others doing loop the loops
Their promises they'll ne'er fulfil
And life is still a treadin' mill

Aye, the day was wet an' getting wetter
Then I received your jaunty letter
Your rhyme was like a breath o' Spring
That made me want tae dance an' sing
And shout out tae that heartless breed
There's a poet born in Fairmileheid

Long may your rhyme aye gie ye pleasure
The gift you have, you aye must treasure
Your thoughts, your dreams and imagination
Write them doon in verse formation
Then Nicky lad you soon will be
A bletherin' Bard, the same as me

I'm proud tae hear you love our City
There's some that don't and more's the pity
But of a' the cities in this world
Fae Canada tae China
Glesga might smile better Nick
But Auld Reekie's that much finer

God bless your Uncle Jim
Cheers
DAVE MANCLARK

26 WINTON TERRACE
EDINBURGH EH10 7AP

13th May 1986

Dear Mr Manclark
I'm glad you wrote a letter
Simply to say
My jaunty wee rhyme
Brightened up your day
But there's something I should mention
To my idol of a sender
That Nicky is a girl
And you got the wrong gender!

I don't blame you really
Not nowadays
When laddies names for lassies
Is the biggest new craze

Davey is Davina
And Wilma is Billie
When Andy is Andrina
They're all rather silly
But of course it works both ways
Both Lindsay and Leslie are now lads
And the most obscure of all
Kerray has joined the new-fankled fads

I have to admit
I've only got myself to blame
My mum christened me Nicola
Which is my proper name
But being a tom-boy
I took the mickey
And changed nice Nicola
To even nicer Nicky!

Yours sincerely
NICKY FISHER

97 Glenvarloch Crescent
Edinburgh EH16 6BB

NICKY IS A LASSIE O'

Fair maid o' Fairmileheid
Apologies for my thoughtless deed
Your letter spun me in a twirl
I'd no idea you were a girl
These new crazes leave me cauld
Maybe 'cause I'm gettin' auld
The sights I see in this guid toon
Make my eyes go birlin' roon

The young yins in their warpaint
And hair a' standin' strecht
Or heids a' shaved like tumshies
Fae foreheid doon tae neck
Their breeks a' torn an' tattered
And belts o' studded brass
I sometimes have tae ponder
Which is lad or lass

I'm reminded o' guid Rabbie's lines
A genius in his day
Did he foresee the future times?
That prompted him tae say

'O wad some power the gift tae gie us
Tae see oorsels as ithers see us
It wid frae many a blunder free us
And foolish notion'

But enough o' a' this tittle tattle
The mair I write, the mair I waffle
I've made a bonnie lassie mad
By thinking Nicky wis a lad
But like a knight on bended leg
Your pardon I sincerely beg
And while I'm on this kneeling limb
Please don't tell your Uncle Jim

So wherever I may wander
No matter where I go
I always will remember
Nicky is . . . a lassie o'

Yours in rhyme
D MANCLARK

THE SAGA O' MONS MEG

Mons Meg is a famous cannon which stands on the Ramparts of Edinburgh Castle, it is made of iron, and was forged in Flanders in the 15th century. According to the records, it is 4.1 metres long (13ft 4ins), and if charged with 47.6 kilos of powder (105lbs) and set at an angle of 45 degrees, it could project an iron ball 1287.5 metres (1408yds) or a stone equivalent, 2621.6 metres (2867yds) which is over a mile and a half, the bore measured .5m (1ft 8ins).

In Fourteen Hundred and Thirty-Nine
The Duke o' Burgundy sipped his wine
Reflecting on his wealth and fame
An idea 'popped' inside his brain

I need a man tae build a Gun
Jean Cambier, will be the one
A Cannon, everyone would prize
A Bombard, o' enormous size

At Mons the giant mould was cast
The carriage fitted hard and fast
The day arrived tae test her bore
And 'Meg' let loose her Birthday roar

Now where in the World, the Duke surmised
Would a Gun like this be idolized
Twas then he heard Auld Scotia's cry
'Freedom an' Liberty, We Do or Die'

Fae Mons tae Lille, fae Lille tae Sloys
Mid sweat an' stour, and muckle noise
And aching limbs, an' clenchit teeth
The 'Great Bombard' was shipped tae Leith

King Jamie's face shone wi' delight
He placed the Gun on the Castle Site
A deterrent o' enormous power
Wid make the bravest hero cower

For the next Two Hundred years an' mair
'Mons Meg' spewed out her bill o' fare
When danger raised it's ugly heid
The 'Iron Murderess' drew her bead

But alas, in Sixteen Eighty-Two
An English gunner joined her crew
He primed a charge tae overload
And caused 'The Bombard' tae explode

Poor 'Meg', she lay, her seams a' burst
Around her Scotsmen, fumed and cursed
Nae mair wid they hear her 'Battle Roar'
Nae mair wid she guard Auld Scotia's shore

For years she lay in dis-repair
The powers that be, just didnae care
They dragged her doon tae London Tower
This once proud Guardian, o' Scotland's Power

Five an' Seventy years went by
Till Wattie Scott, took up the cry
This 'Wizard o' the North' by name
Brought the 'Iron Murderess' hame

Once mair tae Port o' Leith she came
And the Scots were proud tae have her hame
In crowds, the biggest ever seen
They welcomed hame this 'Scottish Queen'

Four tarry-ropes were linked an' tied
Ten braw horses, pranced and shied
A sharp command, they took the strain
Then up 'The Walk', moved this 'Royal Train'

The Third Dragoons, set out the pace
The Bombadiers, were next in place
Then tae the skirl, o' Pipes and Drum
The Highland Seventy-Eight marched on

Banners flew, an' Kirk Bells tolled
As up the Royal Mile she rolled
Cannons roared their Honours blast
Tae this Great Bombard o' the past

They winched her up wi' skilled precision
And placed her in her auld position
Brought hame wi' a' the pomp and grace
'Mons Meg' was BACK IN HER RIGHTFUL PLACE

When gunners meet an' brag their scores
Or cannons blaw their puny roars
In unison they aye recall
The Greatest Cannon of them all. . . 'MONS MEG'

RED, WHITE, OR BLUE

Passion, Pride, and Prejudice
Are a part of every man
Whatever be his colour, race, or creed
They may be lying dormant
Then Fate may change her plan
Eruption, then will follow, no matter what his breed

Then controlled by skillful leaders
Manouvered by their hand
Using and abusing, to succeed
Incensed by their own ego
They will gloriously stand
And watch a once proud Nation, slowly bleed

They'll swear they're democratic
Yet never keep their pledge
Pushing, where the onus is on pull
When faced with opposition
They'll slowly drive their wedge
For those that are divided, cannot rule

There's many look, yet never see
The problems of Society
Never giving what is due
Their own ambitions blind their view

Who knows what other people think
Who cares about their dreams
The thoughts of one ambitious man
Are thoughts enough, it seems

MONUMENTAL REPAIRS

While trauchlin' roon the toon one night
An idea sprang tae mind
I'll daunder doon tae 'Wattie's Howff'
Tae see what I could find
I found him quietly deep in thought
Still sat there on his chair
He smiled in recognition
As I climbed his wee bit stair

'Hello guid friend, you're looking braw
And your 'Hoose' looks good as new
The statuettes are a' in place
Repairs are finally through
Six years have passed an' mair Watt
Since that blether here thon night
I tried tae spread the word aroond
O' your Monumental plight'

'Och it's grand tae see ye Davie man
It's awfy quiet round here
I've never heard a friendly word
Since thon disasterous year
I used tae listen tae the masons
As they chipped away the stane
But they spoke a funny language
That wis different fae our ain'

'They talked o' space invaders
And sounded the alarm
On 'Micro-chips' and 'Trannies'
And 'Bandits' wi' one arm
On 'Video Tapes' and 'Disco'
They'd often disagree
Tae tell ye the honest truth man
It was double dutch tae me'

'And what about your 'lodgers' Watt
Still rowdy and uncouth?'
'Naw, the masons pinned them by the feet
And cemented up their mooths'

'And how about the squirrels Watt
Still scurrying about like mad?
You know I never ever found a trace
O' that tree-load full o' 'yad''

'Aye these squirrels need some watching man
They'll take yer cake an' crumb
But quiz them on their 'Tree o' Bronze'
And they aye go deaf and dumb'

'Your next door neighbour Livingstone
Is he still in the huff?'
'Naw him and I are quite friendly now
But he gets it pretty rough
For every year at Christmas Time
He takes a fair auld towsin'
They build a shed around his feet
It's 'Santa's Temporary Housin''

'And the brand new Waverley Market, Watt
Dae ye think it has some class
Wi' they three marble Dorsal Fins
Set in a sea of glass?'

'Aye the Market looks gey classy man
But it's always my belief
That when dorsal fins show up above
The sharks lie underneath,
But who are we, tae pass our views
Or ken the meaning o' it
I'm jist a chunk o' 'Binnie Stane'
And you're a humble poet'

Well, I took my leave o' Wattie
And began tae clamber doon
When Livingstone turned his head and said,
'Poet Manclark, I presume'
I left them baith there talking
And homeward made my way
Thinking, now that they're sae friendly
I might go back some day.

THE FIRTH OF FORTH

The rivers o' hame, are gie rich in fame
And songs have been sung o' their worth
The 'Queens' have graced, the Clyde's bonnie face
But Kings have sailed up the Forth

GLOSSARY

Aye	Yes or always
A'	All
Auld	Old
Broos	Brows
Bairns	Children
Brig	Bridge
Baith	Both
Bonnie	Pretty
Bletherin'	Talking
Browster Wives	Brewery women
Ba'	Ball
Breeks	Trousers or pants
Birlin'	Whirling or twirling
Braw	Beautiful
Clickit	Clicked
Cairds	Tinkers
Cairter	Cart driver
Close	Alley
Champit neeps	Mashed turnip
Cannae	Cannot
Cuddy	Horse
Ca'd	Called
Cauld	Cold
Cleek	Clique or group
Doon	Down
Dae	Do
Dinnae	Don't
Dram	Double whisky
Dykes	Stone walls
Daundered	Strolled
Dinnae fash yersel	Don't get upset
De'il	Devil
Dumfoonered	Dumfounded
E'er	Ever
Flair	Floor
Fitba	Football
Fae or frae	From
Fu'	Full or drunk
Guid	Good
Gawkin	Staring or gaping
Gies yer patter	Give me your story
Gaun	Going
Gey	Very
Gallus	Daring
Guider	Go-cart
Gird	Hoop
Girnin	Moaning or complaining
Gritter	Road sander

Glossary—*(continued)*

Haud	Hold
Hawker	Pedlar
Hawked	Sold
Hurdie	Wooden cart
Hame	House or home
Intae	Into
Jist	Just
Kith an' kin	Friends and family
Ken	Know
Kyte	Stomach
Lugs	Ears
Laddie	Boy or young man
Lassie	Girl or young lady
Loupin	Leaping or jumping
Lackey man	Servant
Mair	More
Mou'art	Moleskin
Masel	Myself
Mitts	Hands
Nane	None
Nae	No or not
Neeps	Turnips
Nip	Small whisky
Neebors	Neighbours
O'er or owre	Over
Piece an' jam	Bread and jam
Pu'd	Pulled
Peery	Small spinning-top
Peevery beds	Hopscotch
Plate-fy	Plateful
Powny	Pony
Polis	Police
Reek	Smokey smell
Rax't	Stretched or racked
Spag or spug	Sparrow
Sma'	Small
Sautit	Salted
Souk or sook	Suck
Snout	Cigarette (slang)
Skelpin	Smacking or speeding
Skint	No money or broke
Snaw	Snow
Slippit	Slipped
Sae	So
Stour or stoor	Dust
Traisty	Trusty
Tawpies	Foolish women
Tae	To or too
Tattie	Potato
Tattie-peelin' brew	Vodka

Glossary—*(continued)*

Tumshie	Turnip
Teeter	Stagger
Toon	Town
Taen	Taken
Wynd	Alley or close
Wid or wad	Would
Wellies	Rubber boots
Whae	Who
Weel	Well
Zebo	Black grate polish

Printed and Bound in Scotland
by Scotprint Ltd, Musselburgh